St. Nicholas Owen:
Priest-Hole Maker

St. Nicholas Owen: Priest-Hole Maker

Tony Reynolds

GRACEWING

First published in 2014

Gracewing
2 Southern Avenue, Leominster
Herefordshire HR6 0QF

ISBN 978 0 85244 849 6

Typesetting by
Action Publishing Technology Ltd, Gloucester, GL1 5SR

Dedication

To the memory of Philip Caraman, S.J., without whose unceasing work of research, translation and writing this book would not have been possible.

Veritas temporis filia
Truth is the daughter of Time.

Contents

Acknowledgements

I would like to acknowledge the invaluable help and advice given by Fr Thomas McCoog, archivist of the British Province of the Society of Jesus and by Michael Hodgetts the recusant scholar and writer and leading authority on priest-holes.

I would also like to thank the various owners of wonderful and historic Tudor houses for allowing me into their homes to inspect the priest-holes. Similarly, I wish to thank the National Trust and the Catholic Archdiocese of Birmingham for giving me access to the properties they control.

Finally, I wish to acknowledge the great and public-spirited project of providing, at no cost to the reader, out-of-copyright books in online searchable form that has been undertaken by Google Books. As of the time of writing, over 30 million volumes have been scanned, representing an immense aid to scholarship.

List of Illustrations

HENRY VIII

Prologue: The Reformation

There was a time long ago when Christians went in fear of their lives. They met secretly, often after dark, to practice and discuss their faith; arriving and leaving in ones or twos. They arranged hiding places and safe-houses in case they needed to disappear. They took especial care that their neighbours would not guess that they had rejected the old gods, because that would mean they would be denounced to the authorities and that in turn would lead to a painful death in the arena. The Roman historian Tacitus describes the fate that awaited them on capture:

> Nero ... punished with every refinement the notoriously depraved Christians. Their originator, Christ, had been executed in Tiberius' reign by the governor of Judaea, Pontius Pilatus. In spite of this temporary setback, the deadly superstition had broken out again, not just in Judaea (where the mischief had started) but even in Rome. All degraded and shameful practices collect and flourish in the capital.
>
> First, Nero had the self-admitted Christians arrested. Then, on their information, large numbers of others were condemned. ... Their deaths were made amusing. Dressed in wild animals' skins, they were torn to pieces by dogs, or crucified, or made into torches to be set on fire after dark as illumination.

Those times passed and the Christian religion became dominant in Europe. For well over a thousand years the Church prospered and worshippers could practice their faith in security. But then came a

1

time in Tudor England when some Christians had to re-learn the lessons of ancient Rome. They had to worship secretly; to fear informers and to hide in the darkness while their enemies sought them out for interrogation, torture and death.

It is surprising to many that Henry VIII considered himself a Catholic until the day of his death. He defended the traditional doctrines of the Church against the Protestants of the continent and accepted for example the doctrine of transubstantiation – that the Communion wafer and wine are literally transformed into the body and blood of Christ – as well as the necessities of priestly celibacy and confessing one's sins to a priest. All three of these are basic Catholic doctrines which had come under fire from the Protestant movement.

It might be said that the true begetter of the Church of England as we know it today was not Henry, but Thomas Cranmer. Cranmer first came to the King's notice when a courtier told him about a discussion he had had with a young chaplain at Cambridge. Henry was at the time anxious to end his marriage to Catherine of Aragon, and the chaplain had suggested that as there is a verse in Leviticus that forbids marriage between a man and his brother's widow, Henry's marriage was clearly in breach of God's law and a local ecclesiastical court could declare it null and void, so bypassing the Pope completely. When Henry heard this he is said to have declaimed in his customary blunt fashion: 'I will speak to him. Let him be sent for out of hand. This man, I trow, has got the right sow by the ear.'

Things could not be done so simply however, but Cranmer gained the King's respect and a few years later in 1532 Henry appointed him as ambassador to the Holy Roman Empire, a territory centred on what is now Germany and Austria. While stationed there he was exposed to the ideas of the Protestant reformers and came to accept their views. In fact he went so far as to get married to Margarete, the niece of a leading Protestant of Nuremberg, so breaking his priestly vows of celibacy. This had to be kept secret from Henry, and according to a story in *Bishop Cranmer's Recantacyons*, Margarete was smuggled into England in a crate. This seems unlikely, but nevertheless Cranmer was able to keep his marital state unknown to the King for the next fourteen years.

Thomas Cranmer

In 1533 Henry took the momentous decision to defy the Pope and marry Anne Boleyn. Conveniently, the incumbent Archbishop of Canterbury died in that year and Henry was able to appoint Cranmer in his place. This was followed a year later by the passing of the *Act of Supremacy*, declaring that the monarch, and not the Pope, was the head of the Church in England.

A number of other Acts of Parliament was passed over the next three or four years, progressively increasing the separation from Papal rule. They stated for example that canon law was subject to the final agreement of the King, just as with civil law; that the clergy were no longer to remit money to Rome and so on. At first there was relatively little opposition to this. A few prominent people went to the headsman's block, among them John Fisher, Bishop of Rochester, and Thomas More, the Lord Chancellor, but as far as the ordinary worshipper was concerned, he or she came to the same building on Sundays and saw the same priest saying a mass in Latin and expounding the same doctrines as before, apart of course from that declaring the pre-eminence of the Pope. Most people in Tudor times never travelled more than a few miles from the village of their birth and would be extremely vague as to the location of Rome. Seeing little or no difference in practice, it was possible for the congregations and even their parish priests to be at ease with their consciences.

The essential Catholicism of the new Church was affirmed in 1536 by a statement of doctrine known as the *Ten Articles*. Amongst other things, it stated the necessity of infant baptism; that the use of images was acceptable, provided they were not objects of worship; that the sacrament of penance was 'expedient and necessary'; that saints and the Virgin Mary might be honoured, again provided they not be worshipped. Critically, the truth of tran-substantiation was strongly asserted with:

> our people ... ought and must constantly believe, that under the form and figure of bread and wine which we there presently do see and perceive by outward senses, is verily, substantially, and really contained and comprehended the very selfsame body and blood of our Saviour Jesus Christ.

Even this was not considered Catholic enough, so it was followed three years later by the *Six Articles* in which transubstantiation was promoted to being the first point to be affirmed and death by burning specified as the punishment for denying that doctrine.

As Archbishop of Canterbury, Cranmer would have been involved in drafting both of these Acts, but as they uphold doctrines that are anathema to Protestant thinking, including celibacy of the clergy, which he had already violated, and also because we know from a book he published after Henry's death, ingenuously titled *A Defence of the True and Catholic Doctrine of the Sacrament*, that he did not believe that Christ was present in any bodily form in the Communion wafer, it seems that he simply decided it was wiser to defer to the King's views.

The general acquiescence to the new order came under pressure when Henry decided that as he was head of the Church, its lands and property were clearly his own and he could do what he wished with them. Initially, the smaller monastic establishments – those with an income of less than £200 a year – were seized. This process began in 1536.

Almost immediately this led to trouble. Quite apart from the insult seen to be done to holy men and the Church, the monasteries were virtually the only providers of hospitals, education and organised charity. Firstly, there was a rising in Lincolnshire which was brutally put down. This was very soon followed by a larger movement, which became known as the Pilgrimage of Grace. It was centred on York and initially the insurgents expelled the new tenants of the northern religious houses and reinstated the monks and nuns. Their leader was Robert Aske, a London barrister, who later prepared a *Narrative to the King* setting out the reasons for the revolt in which he declared that

> In all parts of the realm men's hearts much grudged with the suppression of abbeys, and the first fruits, by reason the same would be the destruction of the whole religion in England.

At its height, the Pilgrimage of Grace raised forty thousand men and was the greatest threat to his reign that Henry ever faced. If they had marched south, undoubtedly gathering men as they went, they would have raised a force which the King could not match. Henry sent the Duke of Norfolk to negotiate with Aske. Norfolk was authorised to offer a general pardon for the insurgents and agree to allow the abbeys to continue as they were until Parliament had a chance to debate the issue. Aske accepted this and dispersed his men. He was invited to London, where he was won over by Henry's charm and returned to Yorkshire singing the King's praises. Now that the insurgents were scattered, Henry could act and he did so in the most brutal fashion. He had Aske and other ringleaders arrested, tried for high treason and hanged. The abbots of the four largest monasteries in the north were also put to death. At Sawley Abbey, one of the religious houses that had been reinstated by the Pilgrims, the chief monks were 'to be hanged on long pieces of timber, or otherwise out of the steeple.' Five hundred men were hanged at York, Hull and Pontefract alone, many of them being monks and friars in their habits.

The dissolution of the monasteries could now continue without opposition. Convents, friaries and abbeys were emptied. This took

Whitby Abbey

place over four years and caused immense disruption. Many thousands of monks, nuns and lay servants were scattered. In order that communities could not reform, the lead from the roofs was sold off; walls were torn down for building stone and even the doors to the monks' cells were sold. We see the results even today in the many admittedly picturesque ruins of old establishments such as Whitby Abbey (above) and Fountains Abbey.

One great loss was that monastic libraries were destroyed. John Bale, the (Protestant) Bishop of Ossory, wrote mournfully a few years later that:

> A great nombre of them whych purchased those supertycyous mansyons, resrved of those lybrarye bokes, some to serve theyr jakes [lavatories], some to scoure candelstyckes, and some to rubbe their bootes. Some they solde to the grossers and soapsellers.

Throughout all this, the Pope had refrained from taking the final step of formally excommunicating Henry, although this had been threatened after his marriage to Anne Boleyn. The final straw was in 1538 when the shrine of St Thomas Becket at Canterbury was

Henry VIII in his last years

sacked. Thomas' shrine had been considered one of the holiest in
Europe and pilgrims had been flocking to Canterbury for centuries.
The gold and silver offerings were taken to London and were said to
have filled twenty-one wagons. This desecration could not be over-
looked and Pope Paul III issued a Bull of Excommunication against
Henry and Cranmer.

Most of the money from the confiscations was used to finance
Henry's repeated and futile forays into France in an attempt to win
back lands once held by the English crown. Much was also used to
fund his luxurious lifestyle. Henry loved to make a grand show.
Perhaps the most notable example is when a tournament was
organised near Calais ostensibly as a show of friendship with the
French king, Francis I. This was the famous Field of the Cloth of
Gold where Henry was accompanied by 5000 men and gold thread
was woven not only into clothing but even into the tents. Nor did
he stint himself personally: at the beginning of his reign he had
twelve palaces; while at the end of it, by building, seizure or
purchase he had fifty-five.

In 1547, Henry died and was succeeded by his only son who
became Edward VI. He was crowned at the tender age of nine and

reigned only six years before his death. Although it seems that Edward had a genuine interest in religion, given his youth he would have been heavily influenced by his advisors, chief of which was Thomas Cranmer, still Archbishop of Canterbury. Cranmer was enthusiastic about bringing in Protestant changes to the new Church of England. With his influence over the boy-king he was able to make far more sweeping reforms. He oversaw the creation of what is now called the *Book of Common Prayer* to replace the Latin liturgy in use up to that time. This work represented a radical shift towards Protestantism, including having no provision for the vener- ation of the saints; not having prayers for the dead (which would imply the Catholic doctrine of Purgatory); making no provision for private confession and not including a feast day for the Assumption of the Virgin Mary.

The new rubric was extremely unpopular; the laity seeing it as finally representing a clear break with the old religion. There were rebellions in the West Country which were bloodily supressed using an army partly composed of foreign mercenaries. An Act of Parlia- ment, the *Act of Uniformity*, was brought in to deprive of their parishes priests who refused to use the book.

Alas for Cranmer, Edward's reign was short. There was a desperate attempt to enthrone Lady Jane Grey as a reliable and malleable Protestant, but this was short-lived. The country rallied behind Henry's elder daughter, Mary, as the next in line to the throne and Lady Jane lost her head after just nine days of rule.

Mary had endured twenty years of humiliation since her mother, Catherine of Aragon, had been set aside. She herself had been declared illegitimate and had lost her title of princess. She had been lectured by her much younger half-brother, the King, about her religious practices. But now she was the most powerful person in the realm. Mary saw it as her clear duty to return England to Catholicism.

The chances of her achieving her aim seemed reasonably good. Most importantly, the general populace was content with a return to the old faith. As has been pointed out, the Church under Henry was essentially Catholic. The six years of Edward's reign with its violent shift to Protestantism had been met with widespread dismay. In addition, the wider Church had begun a programme of increased discipline which is known as the 'Counter-Reformation'. For example, priests were to be better educated and to be appointed solely on merit and bishops were required to live in their dioceses. These and other steps deprived denigrators of the Catholic Church of many of their arguments.

Mary also had the support of Cardinal Reginald Pole. Pole was the second son of the Countess of Salisbury and had once been an advisor to Henry VIII but had split with him over the matter of the divorce from Catherine of Aragon. He had fled abroad and Henry had spitefully taken his revenge on Pole's family. They were stripped of their titles, lands and money and the Countess was (clumsily: it took eleven strokes of the axe) beheaded. Margaret Pole, as she was at her execution, is regarded as a martyr by the Catholic Church and was later beatified. Cardinal Pole put his abilities and his fervour at Mary's disposal and she made him Archbishop of Canterbury and her chief counsellor.

All the religious laws passed under Edward were repealed. One such law passed a year before his death had allowed priests to marry: any clergy who had taken advantage of this were deprived of their benefices. England once again accepted the religious authority of the Pope.

Cranmer was sent to the Tower as soon as Mary could arrange it. This was closely followed by a trial and a sentence of death. Faced with the bonfire, Cranmer made a complete recantation of his views, affirming the supremacy of the Pope; the truth of transubstantiation and so on. Mary was not however prepared to deal leniently with someone who had been so involved in the betrayal of her religion. She was happy to accept the urging of one of her ambassadors that 'His iniquity and obstinacy was so great against God and your Grace that your clemency and mercy could have no place with him.'

It was perhaps a doubtful decision to require him to make a final statement of contrition on his way to execution. Throwing away the approved script he said that he hadn't meant a word of his previous retractions, 'and as for the pope, I refuse him, as Christ's enemy, and Antichrist with all his false doctrine.' He was dragged from the pulpit and to the stake. Foxe's *Book of Martyrs*, which was written in the reign of Elizabeth to eulogise Protestantism, describes the scene:

Coming to the stake with a cheerful countenance and willing mind, he put off his garments with haste, and stood upright in his shirt: and a bachelor of divinity, named Elye, of Brazen-nose college, laboured to convert him to his former recantation, with the two Spanish friars. And when the friars saw his constancy, they said in Latin to one another 'Let us go from him: we ought not to be nigh him: for the devil is with him.' But the bachelor of divinity was more earnest with him: unto whom he answered, that, as concerning his recantation, he repented it right sore, because he knew it was against the truth; with other words more. Whereby the Lord Williams cried, 'Make short, make short.' Then the bishop took certain of his friends by the hand. But the bachelor of divinity refused to take him by the hand, and blamed all the others that so did, and said, he was sorry that ever he came in his company. And yet again he required him to agree to his former recantation. And the bishop answered, (showing his hand), 'This was the hand that wrote it, and therefore shall it suffer first punishment.'

Fire being now put to him, he stretched out his right hand, and thrust it into the flame, and held it there a good space, before the fire came to any other part of his body; where his hand was seen of every man sensibly burning, crying with a loud voice, *This hand hath offended*. As soon as the fire got up, he was very soon dead, never stirring or crying all the while.

The execution of Cranmer on the nominal charge of treason was to be expected, but the matter for which Mary is generally condemned is the large number of people that she sent to be burnt at the stake for heresy. Several reasons combined to persuade her to follow this policy. Her fervent belief in the rightness of her cause was paramount, fuelled as it had been by years of denigration. She also is likely to have believed that the security of her throne depended on it. In those days the power of the throne and that of religion were inextricably entwined. Opposition to the religion of the ruler was taken as disloyal. Further, it was believed that national unity depended on everyone worshipping in the same way. As the bishop of Chichester put it, 'nothing there is, that breadth so deadly hatred, as diversite of myndes touching religion'. It is sometimes suggested that Cardinal Pole tried to moderate Mary's zeal, but a memoir that he sent to her early in her reign advises her to:

The execution of Thomas Cranmer from Foxe's Book of Martyrs

punish the disobedient in virtue of the authority she has received from God. She must not permit knaves to dare to oppose their own will to their Queen's just intentions, and she must use force to bring about what reason may fail to accomplish.

Mary reigned only five years but in that time she sentenced almost three hundred people to be burnt to death. A notable feature of these executions was that the majority were not preachers or gentlefolk but ordinary working people who refused to recant despite the terrible death that awaited them.

Lewes, the county town of Sussex, was the site of seventeen burnings, and to this day the Gunpowder Plot festivities there are the most fervent in the country: blazing tar barrels are dragged through the street; shouts of 'No Popery!' are raised and finally the Pope, as well as Guy Fawkes, is burnt in effigy.

Fifty-six of those burnt were women. One especially repugnant scene occurred in Guernsey, where three women were executed at once. One of them, Perotine Massey, under the stress of execution

actually gave birth to a boy at the stake. A bystander rescued the
baby, but the bailiff insisted that it too should burn and it was
thrust back into the fire.

If Mary had had enough time and, crucially, had produced an
heir, her campaign might have succeeded. In the event, however, her
reign was short and both she and Cardinal Pole died on the same
day in 1558.

The casual cruelty of Tudor times is alien to the modern mind.
Holinshed's Chronicles states that 72,000 'thieves and rouges' were
hanged in the reign of Henry VIII but both he and his daughter
were products of their times. Specifically, burning at the stake for
heresy was a common procedure: it will be recalled that under
Henry this was the punishment laid down for denying the truth of
transubstantiation. It cannot be denied, however, that there is a
peculiar horror in execution by fire and it is unsurprising that
Mary Tudor is often known by the sobriquet 'Bloody Mary'.

Mary's sister Elizabeth was clearly the next in the line of succession and her accession was not seriously opposed, even though she
had been brought up a Protestant and could be expected to sever the
links with Rome. As the presiding bishop had foretold despairingly
at Mary's funeral: 'The wolves be coming out of Geneva and have
sent their books before, full of pestilent doctrines.'

Elizabeth lost no time in re-instating the *Act of Supremacy*
saying that the monarch was the supreme leader of the Church in
England and requiring the use (with a few minor changes to
appease traditionalists) of the *Book of Common Prayer*. Everyone
was obliged to go to church once a week or be fined twelve pence.
Some writers have described this fine as 'paltry' but we know that
six years earlier when John Dudley needed to raise an army to move
against Mary, he offered ten pence a day to volunteers to serve in
his infantry. It was therefore a significant sum to all but the
wealthy.

Most of the clergy pusillanimously accepted the new order – for
many of them this was after all the fifth set of beliefs they had
embraced – but hundreds refused to do so and were deprived of
their livings. Most of these 'Marian priests' continued to serve in
secret, and for years were the backbone of the Catholic faith.

Elizabeth has a reputation for pursuing what would now be

called a 'don't ask, don't tell' policy with regard to religion. This comes largely from two famous quotations. The first of these, recorded by Francis Bacon, is that she refused to sanction an investigation into whether her subjects were secret Catholics with the words: 'I would not open windows into men's souls.' The other is a remark made late in her reign that 'There is only one Christ, Jesus, one faith. All else is a dispute over trifles.'

A more telling quotation was one she uttered in 1569:

> We know not, nor have any meaning to allow, that any of our subjects should be molested, either by examination or inquisition, in any matter of faith ... so long as they shall in their outward conversation shew themselves quiet and conformable, and not manifestly repugnant to the laws of the realm.

As the 'laws of the realm' included an obligation to attend the state Church this simply meant that it was not unacceptable to be a Catholic, provided one behaved at all times as a Protestant.

On the extreme Protestant wing there was a growing Puritan movement. They had few doctrinal quarrels with the Church of England, but campaigned vigorously for more austere forms of religious ceremony. They considered all images idolatrous; they wanted no ornamentation in church; the priest was not to wear vestments and even the sign of the cross was denounced as 'superstitious.' Unlike Catholics, who were keeping a very low profile, the Puritans were given to vehement preaching against matters they disliked. Elizabeth felt that they too were a threat to good order and attempted to discourage the growth of their beliefs.

There was for a number of years an uneasy truce. The majority conformed to the new faith as outlined by Cranmer and Catholics had a certain amount of freedom, especially in rural areas and the north of the country where the influence of the Crown was weaker. Marian priests ministered to many, although of course their numbers dwindled with time.

Many people had a belief in the old religion, but were worldly enough not to show it. One of the most notorious turncoats of the time was Dr. Andrew Perne, the master of Peterholics College, Cambridge. When he erected a weathervane at his college with his initials at the top, it was jested that these stood for 'A Protestant'; 'A Papist' or 'A Puritan' depending on which way the wind blew. However, he is said to have advised a lady friend in these words:

> You can live in the religion which the Queen and the whole country profess – you will have a good life, you will have none of the vexations which Catholics have to suffer. But don't die in it. Die in faith and communion with the Catholic Church.

It was in this period, the calm before the storm, that Nicholas Owen came to manhood.

ELIZABETH

Young Nicholas

Nicholas Owen was born in Oxford, near the castle, early in the reign of Elizabeth. His father was Walter Owen, a carpenter. We don't know the exact year of his birth, but a witness describing him in late 1605 says he was 'about fifty years of age'[1] which gives a date around 1555. However, we also have the dates of his apprenticeship and unless he began his training rather late in life a more likely date is 1562. No doubt many years of constant travelling in all weathers and hard manual labour had aged him.

Life was often short and always uncertain in those days. When Nicholas was two years old, the Black Death killed one out of seven of the inhabitants of Stratford upon Avon, only fifty miles away. People clung to their families and were fervent in their religion.

It is clear that the Owens embraced the Catholic faith with a passion. We have few records from that date, but we know there were four brothers. The likelihood is that John was the eldest, born in 1561, then Nicholas, then Walter (named after their father) in 1568 and finally Henry in about 1571. All the brothers were to spend their lives, and in Nicholas' case give his life, supporting their Church. The brothers also had a younger sister, Elizabeth.

There is ample evidence that Oxfordshire was reluctant to accept the new order. In 1530 Henry VIII had found it necessary to write to Oxford University complaining about the time they were taking in considering the question of his marriage to Catherine of Aragon. He compared their conduct unfavourably with that of Cambridge which had already sent him the answer he wanted.

Later, in the time of Edward VI, there was a serious uprising in the county caused by several grievances, amongst which was a desire to return to the old Latin services. This was quickly put down and the ringleaders executed. Among these was the vicar of Chipping Norton, who was sentenced to hang in chains from his own church steeple. The young king made an entry in his journal regarding the event:

> To Oxfordshier the Lord Grey of Wilton was sent with 1500 horsemen and footmen; whose coming with th'assembling of the gentlemen of the countrie, did so abash the rebels, that more than hauf of them rann ther wayes, and other that tarried were some slain, some taken and some hanged.[2]

Despite the ferocity of the response, the effects seem to have been limited: at least that is what the Mayor of Oxford thought when he informed the Privy Council in 1561 that 'there were not three houses in [Oxford] that were not filled with Papists.'[3]

This milieu would have made living as Catholics much easier for the Owen family. We do not often hear of recusants (the name given to those that refused to accept the Protestant faith) that were of modest means. The fines and social pressures were much harder to resist if one did not have influence, money and servants. The fact that the Owens were able to survive indicates that they had friends or sympathisers as neighbours and as officials of their local parish, St Peter le Bailey. Fines were collected at a local level based on lists compiled by the churchwardens of non-attendants at services. The fact that they were not beggared suggests that their names were not recorded.

In 1566, with his wife and the two children born to date, Walter moved to No. 3 Castle Street, which he leased from Magdalen College. Overshadowing their home was the Norman castle itself. The illustration opposite was made a century earlier, but it would have looked much the same to the Owen family. Castle Street is to the east of the site: roughly opposite the view shown.

We know from the inventory in his Will that the ground floor contained Walter's workshop and day rooms, with the bedrooms on the upper floor. Nicholas would surely have helped his father at his

Oxford Castle in the 15th Century

work and got to know the trade. As much of a carpenter's work is concerned with building, he would also have visited building sites with his father and done some fetching and carrying. Given his youth and short stature his help may have been limited but he would have become familiar with the principles of construction, and this was to serve him well in future years.

A few years later in 1570, attitudes to religion hardened on both sides. It was in that year that Pope Pius V issued a Bull known, as is customary, by its opening words: *Regnans in Excelsis* ('Ruling from on high') attacking Elizabeth. The most important paragraph ran:

> We do declare Her to be deprived of her pretended Title to the Kingdome aforesayd, and of all Dominion, Dignity, and Priviledge what soever; and also the Nobility, Subjects, and People of the sayd Kingdome, and all others which have in any sort sworne unto Her, to be for ever absolved from any such Oath, and all manner of duty of dominion, alleageance, and obedience.

In other words, Elizabeth was not a legitimate queen and the people of England should reject her authority.

Elizabeth's immediate reaction was to bring in further laws to frustrate any attempts to undermine her authority. The *Treasons* Act made it high treason to affirm that the queen ought not to enjoy the Crown, or to declare her to be a heretic. Another Act made it high treason to bring objects blessed by the Pope into England.

Elizabeth was also feeling vulnerable because Mary Queen of Scots was her prisoner and the nearest in the line of succession to the throne. Mary, a Catholic, became a focus for disaffection and several plots to overthrow Elizabeth were centred on her. All these matters contributed to an increase in tension.

When he grew to manhood John Owen decided to study at Oxford University. He first entered Corpus Christi, then moved to Trinity where he graduated in 1580. In theory, this should have been impossible because graduands were required to take an oath recognising Elizabeth as head of the Church. In practice, Trinity College was run by the formidable Lady Elizabeth Pope, the wife of the founder, who was a staunch Catholic and used her right of making all appointments at the college to ensure that it was populated by men of a like mind. No doubt the requirement to take the oath was quietly waived. A couple of years later, John became a tutor at Trinity and was able to help his younger brother Walter become a student there at the tender age of thirteen.

It may be noted that matters were very different at other colleges, where even ten years earlier one Catholic had ruefully noted that 'No one could enter a university unless he was or pretended to be a heretic.'[4]

It was around this time that the Catholic Church began a programme of building seminaries on the continent to train native Englishmen as priests. There would obviously be no point in sending foreign-born missionaries – their accents would betray them at once. The English College at Douai in the Low Countries was the first to be established, and later there were others in Spain, France and Italy. The Marian priests were getting older and there was a clear need for a younger generation to keep the faith alive. Graduates of these colleges were known as 'seminary priests' and it was on them that the main persecution was to fall. Both John and

Walter went to Douai to train as priests in the year 1583 when John was twenty-three, and Walter only fifteen.

It must have become clear early on that Nicholas was very short. All his life he was referred to as 'Little John' or 'Little Michael.' We don't know his exact height, but we do know the average height of a man of that time. One of the best indications of this comes from the recovery in modern times of Henry VIII's warship the *Mary Rose* which sank in front of him at Portsmouth. The skeletons of the sailors on board were preserved in the mud of the Solent and so we know that their height averaged 5 foot 7 inches. Nicholas must have been a good deal shorter than this to deserve his cognomen but on the other hand we know he was able to ride a horse and carry out heavy mason's work. We can guess that he was 5 foot tall or a little less, but strongly built.

It is certain that Nicholas would have considered following the example of his brothers, but at that time men with handicaps were not acceptable for the priesthood. The Church took literally the words of Leviticus on the selection of priests, which included the instruction that:

> No man who has any defect may come near: no man who is blind or lame, disfigured or deformed; no man with a crippled foot or hand, or who is hunchbacked or dwarfed.

His exceptionally short stature is likely to have disqualified him, and he perforce needed to learn a trade. This in turn meant that he had to serve a period of apprenticeship. The *Statute of Artificers* in force at that time insisted that all tradesmen serve an apprenticeship of at least seven years. In the words of the Act:

> It shall not be lawful to any person or persons other than such as now do lawfully exercise any art, mystery or manual occupation to set up, occupy, use or exercise any craft, mystery or occupation now used or occupied within the realm of England or Wales except he shall have been brought up seven years at least as an apprentice in manner or form above said.

To enforce this it also declared it illegal to employ a tradesman who had not served such an apprenticeship. On the completion of his apprenticeship, which was often crowned with the production of a test piece, the young man became a journeyman and could seek employment in his craft and in time perhaps become a master himself.

It might have been supposed that Nicholas would follow his father into carpentry, but in fact he chose to become a joiner. It is important to recognise the difference between the two trades. A carpenter at that time would have been largely concerned with house building, where the highest precision and finish is not necessary. A carpenter might indeed construct simple, nailed furniture, but nothing that required a perfect finish. A joiner on the other hand built quality furniture and fabricated other things such as wainscoting: the wooden wall-panelling that was so popular in Tudor times. Because these things displayed their owners' wealth, millimetric accuracy and a perfect finish was required. Nailing was relatively rare – the pieces were fastened together with tight-fitting mortice and tenon joints or dovetails and set in glue. It was the skills he learnt in these years that enabled Nicholas to do the work for which he is famous.

Nicholas Owen enrolled as an apprentice to the Oxford joiner William Conway on February 2, 1577. His papers of indenture run as follows:

Memorandum that on the third day of February in the nineteenth year of the reign of Lady Elizabeth by the Grace of God Queen of England, France and Ireland Nicholas Owen son of Walter Owen citizen of Oxford carpenter placed himself as an apprentice to the art of William Conway, citizen of the above, joiner, etc. from the feast of the purification of Blessed Mary last past before the present date until the final end of the full completion of the eight years following etc. And he will give to the same Apprentice sixteen pence of good and legal money during the aforesaid term at the four feast[s] of the year namely at Easter, Pentecost of the Lord, St Michael the Archangel and the Nativity of the Lord in equal portions. At the end of the said eight years he will give to his same Apprentice two such sets of clothes suitable for his apprenticeship and ten shillings of good and legal English money and twelve implements belonging to his said art at the aforesaid time of office.[5]

Working at the lathe in Tudor times

When Nicholas was in the third year of his apprenticeship, an important challenge to the established order was issued by another Oxford man, Edmund Campion. Although he initially accepted Protestant principles, Campion had a crisis of conscience at the age of twenty-nine and entered the English College at Douai to train as a priest, following which he travelled to Rome and was accepted into the Jesuit order. In 1580 he was sent to England to work for the Catholic faith. In the following year he caused a stir by issuing a short statement setting out his mission, known as the *Challenge to the Privy Council*, or, *Campion's Brag*. Defiantly, he closed with the words:

And touching our Society, be it known to you that we have made a
league – all the Jesuits in the world, whose succession and multitude
must overreach all the practice of England – cheerfully to carry the
cross you shall lay upon us, and never to despair your recovery, while
we have a man left to enjoy your Tyburn, or to be racked with your
torments, or consumed with your prisons.

A posthumous portrait of Campion is shown below – the noose and
knife indicate the manner of his death.

A short time later he published his book *Decem Rationes* ('Ten
Reasons'), arguing against the validity of the Church of England. It
was printed clandestinely and to great scandal copies were found on
the benches at a degree ceremony at the University church of St
Mary's, Oxford. At that time John Owen was at Trinity College a
short walk away. John was not directly involved in this (the books
were smuggled in by Father William Hartley who helped Campion
with printing and distribution) but he would have been fully aware
of the prank.

His high profile made Campion a magnet for Catholics and when
he was at an inn just outside Oxford a group of students and tutors
implored him to preach to them. Although we have no confirmation

Edmund Campion

of this, as pious Catholics it is very plausible that the Owen brothers were in this party. Campion did not dare preach in so public a place but agreed to do so the next Sunday at Lyford Grange, the home of a local recusant gentleman. In the congregation on that occasion was a government spy, George Elliott. He sent a message to a local Justice of the Peace and a few hours later the house was invaded by fifty armed men. Campion and his two chaplains were hurried to a priest-hole. The search went on all Sunday afternoon and well into the night and involved much smashing of walls and panelling. They began again the next morning and were losing hope of finding anyone, when, as described in a contemporary document, they came to:

> A chamber near the top of the house, which was but very simple, having in it a large great shelf with divers tools and instruments both upon it and hanging by it, which they judged to belong to some cross-bow maker. The simpleness of the place caused them to use small suspicion in it and they were departing out again; but one in the company [David Jenkins] by good hap espied a chink in the wall of boards whereto this shelf was fastened, and through the same he perceived some light. Drawing his dagger he smit a great hole in it, and saw there was a room behind it, whereat the rest stayed, searching for some entrance into it, which by pulling down a shelf they found, being a little hole for one to creep in at.[6]

Jenkins called out loudly: 'I have found the traitors.' and Campion and his companions were arrested.

Taken to the Tower of London he was tortured for about four months, then tried and convicted of the ridiculous charge of plotting to murder the Queen. For this he was sentenced to be hanged, drawn and quartered. That is; strangled at the end of a rope until just short of death, then castrated and disembowelled, and lastly beheaded and dismembered.

A famous histrionic speech on the matter sets out the good reasons behind each step:

> for that he hath been retrograde to Nature, therefore is he drawn backward at a Horse-Tail. And whereas God hath made the Head of Man the highest and most supreme Part, as being his chief Grace

The Quartering Block

and Ornament he must be drawn with his Head declining downward, and lying so near the Ground as may be, being thought unfit to take benefit of the common Air.

For which Cause also he shall be strangled, being hanged up by the Neck between Heaven and Earth, as deemed unworthy of both, or either; as likewise, that the Eyes of Men may behold, and their Hearts contemn him.

Then he is to be cut down alive, and to have his Privy Parts cut off and burnt before his Face, as being unworthily begotten, and unfit to leave any Generation after him. His Bowels and inlay'd Parts taken out and burnt, who inwardly had conceived and harboured in his heart such horrible Treason.

After, to have his Head cut off, which had imagined the Mischief. And lastly, his Body to be quartered, and the Quarters set up in some high and eminent Place, to the View and Detestation of Men, and to become a Prey for the Fowls of the Air.[7]

The success of Campion's efforts led to yet another increase in tension. Yet more Acts of Parliament were promulgated against Catholics. In the year of his execution, the *Act to retain the Queen's Majesty's subjects in their obedience* was passed. This made it high treason to convert to Catholicism – called in the Act the 'Romish religion' – or to convert another person to the faith. It also imposed a fine of 100 marks and a year's imprisonment on anyone attending Mass. A mark was 160 pence or 13s 4d, so 100 marks was over £66 – an impossible sum.

Even after this was law, the Earl of Leicester wrote that 'Her Majesty is slow to believe that the great increase of Papists is of danger to the realm. The Lord of His mercye open her eyes.'[8] His prayer seems to have been answered, for in 1585 Parliament passed an *Act against Jesuits, Seminary priests and other such like disobedient persons*. This made it high treason for any seminary priest to be in England at all and also for anyone to shelter them. It was under this law that many priests were to die.

It's at this point that there is a long-standing myth regarding Nicholas' career. It has its origin in a collection of short biographies of Jesuit martyrs published in 1675 by Mathias Tanner having the title: *Societas Jesu usque ad Sanguinis et Vitae Profusionem Militans* ('The Society of Jesus Fighting to the Outpouring of Blood and Life') and is often referred to as Tanner's *Martyres*. This book was very popular in its day probably because its subject matter was considered devotional, but unlike most devotional works it made an exciting read as it described adventures and narrow escapes culminating in martyrdom. Each biography was headed by an engraving showing the method of execution, including hanging, drowning, beheading, racking, disembowelment and so on.

In his book, Tanner states that Nicholas (presumably having abandoned his apprenticeship) was a servant of Campion's at that time and that on Campion's arrest he made 'free, public and open praise' of his master which earned him a period of imprisonment.

Tanner rarely left his native Bohemia so to compile his work he was dependent on collecting information from others and therefore his accounts are occasionally unreliable. In this particular case he also was writing long after anyone who knew Nicholas was dead. It is now believed that he mis-identified a prisoner in the Bridewell jail named as 'John' (not 'Little John') who had been imprisoned because 'he let fall some words in praise of [Campion]'.[9] In fact this prisoner was John Jacob, an Oxford musician who had been arrested with Father Campion at Lyford Grange.

Further confirmation of the error is given by a brief note in a history of the Jesuits by Henry More. More was an Englishman and his account predates *Martyres* by fifteen years. He states that Nicholas was tortured and killed by the authorities 'when he fell into their hands for the second time.'[10] We have contemporary records of an arrest in 1594, which would have been his first imprisonment.

Tanner also says that in prison Nicholas added punishments of his own and always wore a hair-shirt to mortify the flesh. A hair-shirt was woven out of goat's hair and was therefore itchy and uncomfortable. These were worn almost as a matter of course by priests of that time, but it would not have been expected of a servant and as there is no other indication in contemporary accounts of Nicholas wearing one, we can regard it as doubtful.

At about the time Nicholas would have completed his apprenticeship in 1585, his brother John, now ordained as a priest, was sent back to England to begin his apostolate. The younger brother Walter, who would have been considered too young for ordination, stayed on the continent. He was later sent to the newly-opened seminary at the English College in Valladolid, Spain and died there in 1591.

John's service did not start well. He was captured within the year and imprisoned in the Marshalsea. He was tried and sentenced to death and in order to save his life he took the Oath of Supremacy accepting that the monarch and not the Pope was head of the Church. We can however be certain that his recantation was not sincere, because ten years later in 1596, a priest wrote to his superior praising Nicholas and saying: 'If money is offered him by way of payment he gives it to his two brothers: one of them is a priest, the other a layman in prison for his faith.'[11] The writer was Father Henry Garnet, whom he was to serve until they both were put to death.

Nicholas' youngest brother, Henry Owen, elected to become a printer. This was a promising trade at the time, especially at

Oxford, where the needs of the University were growing. It was in that period that Oxford University decided that it needed its own printer, and in 1586 it arranged for a press to be set up with a chief printer, Joseph Barnes, and one apprentice.[12] This marked the modest beginnings of what became the Oxford University Press, now the largest academic press in the world.

A book issued towards the end of Henry's career records that he had been apprenticed to Barnes.[13] But further, Henry must have been the very first apprentice at the Press. An apprenticeship was normally for seven or eight years, and the same book also states that Henry was in the Clink prison in London nine years after Barnes started his work. It seems therefore that when Barnes started up as a printer (he was already a bookseller) he took on Henry to assist him. The illustration below shows one of the first books from the press. Henry would have helped produce this. When Henry became a journeyman

The title page of Sphaera Civitatis (The Sphere of State) by John Case

he must have begun to clandestinely print Catholic books and pamphlets on the instructions of the priests he worked for, but was soon caught and imprisoned.

Father Henry Garnet has been introduced above. In his youth Henry Garnet, like Henry Owen, had served an apprenticeship with a printer. Later, he journeyed to Rome where he became a priest in the Society of Jesus (the Jesuits). He was sent to England as part of a mission, landing at an isolated spot near Folkestone in 1586 with his friend and companion the priest-poet Robert Southwell. The Jesuit Superior at that time, William Weston, assigned him to the Midlands where there was a shortage of priests and arranged for him to be based at the home of a wealthy recusant family with which Weston was friendly. This place was the manor house in the village of Shoby, Leicestershire and was at that time occupied by two ladies: the young widow Eleanor Brooksby and her unmarried sister Anne Vaux. The Vaux sisters will appear again and again in this narrative: they were the daughters of Lord William Vaux who had been imprisoned and heavily fined for harbouring Edmund Campion. Garnet and Nicholas were to move constantly from house to house to evade their pursuers and almost always the Vaux family would arrange to buy, rent or even build premises where they could find shelter and would usually live there themselves to provide cover.

Southwell was assigned to London at a house in Hackney also owed by Lord Vaux. It was Southwell's job to meet new seminary priests, shelter and instruct them in their duties, then despatch them to where they were needed. A year later, with advice and assistance from Garnet, he started a clandestine printing press.

Father Garnet had very little time to settle into his assignment: within three weeks of his landing, Weston was captured and, following instructions laid down earlier by the Jesuit General, Garnet himself became the leader of the Jesuits in England. During the rest of his career, Garnet is often referred to as the 'Provincial' which is the title given to the senior member of an ecclesiastical order in a given region. Strictly speaking however this was not correct as England and Wales was not at that time designated a 'Province.'

Having suddenly become the Superior, Henry Garnet felt that his

first task should be to acquaint himself with the situation throughout the country. Accordingly, he set out on a long tour of northern
England visiting, as we believe, Yorkshire, Nottinghamshire and
Derbyshire. The journey took about five months and covered several
hundred miles.[14]

It is not known for certain how Garnet came to meet Nicholas.
Some have put forward the theory that Garnet had contacted Henry
Owen in connection with the covert press Garnet and Southwell
were setting up and through him met Nicholas but, as we have seen,
Henry was only starting his apprenticeship as a printer at that time
and would not have been an authority. Most likely, Nicholas came
to London to visit his brother John in prison and met Garnet there
ministering to other imprisoned Catholics; Marshalsea being the
main holding prison for recusants. They would have become
acquainted and Garnet would have been assured that Nicholas was
trustworthy and presumably offered him a job in his service.

The date he started his service is also not precisely known. Father
John Gerard, one of the main sources we have from that time, said
variously: 'For nearly twenty years he had been Father Garnet's
companion'[15] and: 'This man did for seventeen or eighteen years
continually attend upon Father Garnett.'[16] However, there is a
correction in the original manuscript of the latter which shows that
Gerard originally wrote 'eighteen or nineteen.' Therefore we can be
sure that Gerard gave some thought to this and, given the date of
Nicholas' death in 1606, we arrive at the years 1588 or 1589. As
Garnet spent a lot of time in London in the former year to deal with
the problems caused by the advent of the Spanish Armada, 1588 is
perhaps the more likely date.

This was a pivotal point in Nicholas Owen's life. His apprenticeship would have ended three years previously and no doubt he was
making a good living as a tradesman in the prosperous town of
Oxford. He abandoned this secure environment, where he had been
born and had grown up with his parents, family and friends, for a
life of constant danger. As someone who would 'relieve, comfort, aid
or maintain' a Jesuit he became liable to death as a traitor. We can
only speculate what caused him to take this path, but the most
powerful reason must have been a burning desire to help the
Catholic cause. Two of his brothers were already in the priesthood

and the third was training to print necessary literature to support the work of priests and Nicholas must have felt that it was his duty to do more to assist his Church in those dark days. Garnet's offer of employment was his chance to aid the faith and he decided to take it.

So it was that Nicholas became Henry Garnet's servant and assistant and worked with him to minister to those who had remained faithful to the Catholic religion.

ARMADA

The Bloody Question

In piecing together events which occurred almost half a millennium ago, we are fortunate in having a number of primary sources. An important one for this narrative is a remarkable document written by the Jesuit priest Father John Gerard. He comes into this story often because the period of time he worked in England closely matches that of Nicholas Owen's service and their paths cross regularly. After spending eighteen years in his apostolate he managed to escape to the Continent where he was set to training novices for their assignments. His superiors ordered him to write an account of his work and this story — usually referred to as his *Autobiography* — with its account of hair-breadth escapes, daring rescues, torture and fearful crouching in priest-holes while the pursuivants tore down walls to find him, is as gripping as any thriller.

The other important source for this book is the letters of Father Garnet. Most of these were to his superior, the Jesuit Father General in Rome, Claudio Aquaviva. Garnet wrote two or three letters a year to him to report on progress and make requests. He sent these to Rome via the Spanish ambassador in London (later, when England was at war with Spain, the Venetian ambassador) and most of them still exist in the Jesuit archives, as do copies of the replies that were sent. His letters are dated but because of the danger of interception he does not normally mention specific places, saying for example that he was in the 'diocese of Worcester'. However, from our knowledge of recusant houses and the incidents he describes we

31

Henry Garnet

are able to build up a fair picture of his movements, and therefore of the movements of Nicholas. Garnet also tends not to mention names unless they have died or been executed, but again we can make informed deductions.

We also have a few letters that Garnet wrote to friends overseas and some from prison that were intercepted by the authorities and so have survived.

Another primary source is the records of the English College at Douai, known as the *Douai Diaries*. These are invaluable in giving us specific information on which priests were trained and sent out and much other information relating to the persecution.

For events towards the end of Nicholas' life, we have two parallel documents which appear to have been based on the same original, now lost, manuscript. One is a translation by Gerard known as the *Narrative of the Gunpowder Plot* or simply the *Narrative*. The other is *The Gunpowder Plot: The Narrative of Oswald Tesimond alias Greenway*. Tesimond was a Jesuit priest who was at school in York with Guy Fawkes and other young men who were later to be involved in the Gunpowder Plot, and with Edward Oldcorne who also became a Jesuit and returned to England on his mission with John Gerard. These documents deal more specifically with the events surrounding the plot to blow up parliament and include some detailed information about Nicholas.

When Garnet took over as Superior, he accepted something of a poisoned chalice. In the last five years of Weston's service more than 150 priests had been sent to England from the colleges at Douai and Rome but only about one in three of these was still alive and free.[1] The rest had been executed, died of natural causes, fled back to the Continent, or were languishing in prison. As it took six or seven years to train a priest, this was a disastrous rate of attrition.

These priests were in the main 'secular clergy' who did not belong to any specific religious order. Weston, Garnet and Southwell, however, were members of the Society of Jesus, the only ecclesiastical order in England at that time. Garnet was 'leader' therefore of exactly one priest – his friend Southwell. They were the only Jesuits in England at the time not in prison.

It is hardly surprising that Garnet's overwhelming requirement was for more help. 'I implore your Paternity and in the most earnest manner, send us a supply of priests as quickly as you possibly can,'[2] he wrote to his superior. Aquaviva responded, and the number of priests despatched on their mission increased sharply. Being sent, however, did not mean they would arrive. Getting the seminary priests safe to London so that they could be deployed where they were needed was fraught with difficulties. It had been known for some years that the Spanish were preparing the Armada and precautions were being taken by the authorities. The government had arranged that watchers were placed to accost strangers on roads from the coast, and had even placed spies in French ports. We can take as an example the adventures of Father Gerard when he first arrived in England from the seminary in Rome.

He relates that he took ship for England with three other priests, one of them Edward Oldcorne as mentioned above. He describes it as a 'lucky load', except as regards himself, because the other three were eventually captured and executed and so gained 'the crown of martyrdom'. The ship's boat put them ashore at a quiet point on the

Norfolk coast after dark. They tried to find a path inland but every track led to a farm where the dogs began to bark. Accordingly, they spent a sleepless night sheltering from the rain in a wood. At dawn they separated and Gerard walked a short distance before he met some country folk. He walked up to them boldly and claimed to be a falconer who had lost his bird and was wandering around in search of it. With this cover, he was able to wander around the hedges and lanes and got well away from the sea. Gerard was fortunate in that, having been brought up as a gentleman, he was able to talk about such matters as hunting and falconry and so allay suspicion. In fact his favourite disguise for his entire stay in England was just that – a gentleman of moderate degree.

At the end of the day he was about nine miles away from the sea and entered an inn for the night. In the morning he bought a pony and started out in the direction of Norwich. After only two miles he encountered a group of watchers at the entrance to a village. They made him dismount and questioned him. Gerard claimed to be in the service of an eminent man and again used his lost hawk story. They were not satisfied with this and insisted he come with them to talk to the Constable and Officer of the Watch. Both unfortunately at that time happened to be hearing a church service and Gerard was not prepared to enter a church he regarded as heretical even in such circumstances. 'Go and tell the officer,' he said, 'that if he wants to see me, either he must let me wait for him here or come out quickly.' The officer came out in a suspicious mood and questioned Gerard closely. He could not catch him out in his replies and threat-ened to take him before a Justice of the Peace. In the end, however, he relented and said: 'You've got the look of an honest fellow. Go on then in God's name.'

Later that day, getting near Norwich, he had the luck to fall in with a simple young country man and chatting to him found out a number of things that would be useful in any future questionings and also obtained directions to an inn which he could get to without riding through the town. At that inn he began talking with other guests and in the course of conversation had a man pointed out to him as a stubborn Papist. Later he approached that man and confessed to being a priest and asked for his help. This man intro-duced him to a wealthy Catholic who gave him a horse and a servant so he could complete his journey to London and report to Garnet, so (with Oldcorne who had already arrived) boosting the number of Jesuits under his control to three.

It can be seen from this that just entering the country was a dangerous undertaking. In this party alone, two of the four priests were captured and later executed before they could even start work.

Once priests had been assigned to their duties, there was a continuing problem of how to hide them in the event of a raid. It was often used against them that priests always based themselves in the homes of rich families. In fact, of course, this was inevitable. It was only in a large and rambling house that it would be possible to construct hiding places. Servants could also be called upon to give warning of a raid and help with concealment, and money was often useful in buying off trouble.

At that time hiding places were few and badly built. William Weston, Garnet's predecessor as Jesuit Superior, had had recourse to a priest-hole a few years before. He had just said Mass at a recusant household when there was a raid. A servant rushed up to his room and ushered him to a hiding-place underground. The pursuivants searched for two days but didn't find him, although on occasions they got very close. 'Catholic houses have several places like this, otherwise there would be no security,' he writes, but marvels that 'It was astonishing that men like this, skilled in their task, should fail to find a place that was constructed with no particular cunning or ingenuity.'[3] Even though he escaped, the hide was dank and cold and so narrow that he was forced to stand for the whole time.

Indeed, most priest-holes were not made to withstand a determined search. Very often a corner of a loft or other room would be enclosed by a lath-and-plaster screen, easily detectable by measurement or simply by knocking and listening for hollow sounds. As we have seen, Father Campion was taken because his hide was so badly built that light could be seen through the cracks.

Now that the persecution was intensified, matters had to improve. The authorities were regularly raiding the houses of recusants. Any weapons not clearly necessary for the defence of the premises were confiscated and if the presence of a priest was suspected a rigorous search, including the breaking down of walls, would ensue.

In May 1588 the Armada sailed as a fleet of 151 ships. It engaged the English navy under Sir Francis Drake two months later and was famously defeated. Spain was at that time the most powerful country in the world with vast territories and immense wealth arriving from the New World and the fact that it could be so roundly defeated by the English was taken as a clear sign of God's favour of the Protestant cause. A pageant was organised culminating in a great thanksgiving service at St Paul's. A commemorative medal was struck bearing the words: *Flavit Jehovah et Dissipati Sunt* – God Blew and They Were Scattered.

The events were even the subject of a deck of playing cards. The knave of hearts depicted opposite shows Pope Sixtus V agreeing to contribute towards the expenses of the fleet. (The money was to be given following a successful invasion, so in the event Sixtus did not have to pay.)

The most tragic consequence of the Armada's coming was that in the eyes of the ordinary person it had linked the Catholic religion with enmity towards England. Not only had the Pope promised money, but he had blessed the banner of the fleet before it sailed. The ships had almost 200 priests aboard to hear confessions and say masses. The Pope had even made arrangements for an English-born priest, William Allen, to assume the post of Archbishop of Canterbury. Allen prepared a pamphlet for distribution after the Spanish had landed. In intemperate language it attacked Elizabeth as 'an incestuous bastard, begotten and borne in sinne, of an infamous courtesan Anne Bullen, afterward executed for aduoutery, heresie and incest.'[4] Given all this, it was now easy and plausible for preachers to denounce all Catholics as traitors and there was a marked change in the attitude of conforming citizens towards those that clung to the old faith. In the past there had been much sympathy and tolerance for those that simply wanted to worship in the old way, but that attitude changed abruptly. In fifty years the Catholic Church had gone from being the beloved and unquestioned religion of England to being the creed of traitors that wished to depose the Queen and impose foreign rule upon the country.

When a priest was captured, the question would be put to him: 'What would you do if the Pope were to send over an army and declare that his only object was to bring the kingdom back to its

The Pope Consulting with his Cardinalls & Contributing a million of Gold towards the Charge of the Armada —

An 'Armada' playing card

Catholic allegiance? Whose side would you be on then – the Pope's or the Queen's?' This was an impossible question for any Catholic, who normally fell back on declaring that the matter would never arise. It became known as the 'Bloody Question' because anyone who was not able to deny the Pope's authority was perforce a traitor and subject to the penalty of death. It was especially difficult for Jesuits who, in addition to the vows of poverty, chastity and obedience taken by all priests, take a fourth vow of special obedience to the Pope. As well as this, the fact that their order had been founded by a Spaniard and was especially strong in Spain made them a focus of suspicion. Whereas no priests at all had been executed in England in the previous eight months, now in the months of August to November alone of the Armada year, seventeen priests were put to death. The attitude of the mob against Catholics reached a frenzy. Robert Southwell wrote to Aquaviva bewailing that 'The hatred stored up against the Spaniards they are wreaking with a sort of bestial fury upon their own fellow citizens.'[5]

The Armada was an important reason for Garnet to shift the centre of his operations to London. It was there that he could be at the centre of things and get the latest intelligence and forward it to Rome. Before this time he had been writing to his superior a couple of times a year but in the latter half of 1588 he was sending his reports almost monthly. It was therefore necessary for him to find a secure base in London. He would have been welcome at a number of houses of wealthy recusants, but these were usually well known to the authorities and were in constant danger of being raided. He finally fixed on a house to the north of the City of London, in Finsbury Fields. The houses there were relatively isolated but close to the Moor Gate entrance through the City wall. He decided for greater security to give the impression that the house was unoccupied. In that way he could avoid the attentions of officials who would regularly check premises to ensure that all the occupants were attending divine service. As he reported some years later to Aquaviva, he gave orders that those living there were not to speak even in:

> a natural voice for fear of being over-heard in the road hard by. Nor was it permissible in the daytime to prepare food or to light a fire even in the most bitter winter weather for fear the smoke might be seen. All food was cooked by night and eaten cold the next day.[6]

Visitors were not to come in daylight. It was in these conditions that Nicholas would have lived.

It can be imagined that Nicholas did not have an easy life in his first few months as Garnet's servant. In the winter of that year life in a house without a fire must have been very uncomfortable. Nicholas would have been responsible for cooking the meals at night and serving them the next day. Presumably washing and somehow drying clothes, running errands, taking messages and performing

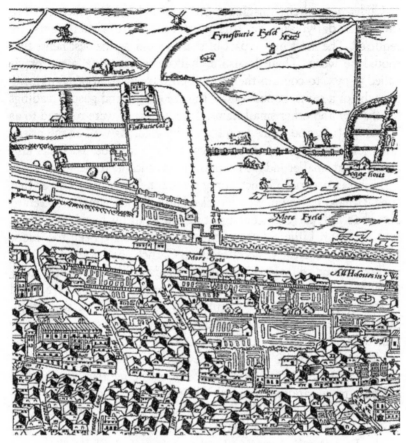

Finsbury Fields and the Moor Gate to London

all the uncounted menial tasks required. When Garnet was on the road, which as we shall see was very frequent, Nicholas would have the extra tasks of loading the horses and then unpacking the goods at the end of the journey. It is also very likely that he assisted with the printing press which Robert Southwell was running at another location.

It was in this house that Nicholas built what was probably his first priest-hole. It was in the cellar behind an untidy store of beer barrels, fuel and provisions and could accommodate six or seven men.

Under normal circumstances, every Catholic priest is expected to say Mass daily, and for this purpose certain ritual items are required. The most bulky part of these would be the vestments that should be worn. There is also a chalice for the wine, a receptacle called a 'pyx' to contain the Host, a portable altar stone containing the relic of a saint, books containing the epistle and gospel readings for the day and other small items. Together these were referred to as 'massing stuff' and formed a quite bulky load. As well as the priest-holes for human occupancy for which he is famous, Nicholas also constructed smaller hides to contain items such as these.

Nicholas was not Garnet's only assistant. There was also at that time Richard Fulwood, who handled administrative matters. Gerard described him as '[Garnet's] agent in nearly all his business.'[7] There was also John Lillie, who sounds as if he may have been the Tudor equivalent of a creative accountant as Garnet once praised his skill in 'buying and selling without taxes.'[8] This is, however, likely to be code for organising the sending of young men overseas and receiving priests into the country. In addition, there was Hugh Sheldon who seems, with Nicholas, to have carried out manual work rather than having the clerical duties of Fulwood and Lillie.

Garnet had now to assign his new priests to their duties. Before the end of 1588 Gerard was sent back to the gentleman who had helped him on landing: Edward Yelverton of Grimston, near King's Lynn. Garnet provided him with clothes and money so that he wouldn't be a burden to his host. His responsibility was to minister to the East Anglian region. In the spring of the following year, Garnet accompanied Edward Oldcorne to Hindlip House in Worcestershire, the home of Thomas Habington, and left him there to build up a religious centre for the west of England. Hindlip became famous for its innumerable priest-holes and it's probable that Nicholas took the opportunity to build at least one on this visit so that Oldcorne would have a place of concealment in the event of a raid. Oldcorne was to stay at Hindlip for the next seventeen years.

BRADDOCKS

Refuge

In the year following the Armada, the frenzied persecution of Catholics eased. In fact not a single Catholic was executed in London in 1589. Added to this, the number of young men arriving from the seminaries abroad reached new levels. Almost forty newly-ordained priests had entered the country from Douai and the English College in Rome and had survived the dangerous journey to London.[1] About five of these were Jesuits, so Father Garnet now had a usefully-sized corps at his disposal. Priests were being deployed around the country and Nicholas was kept busy building priest-holes for them. This must have occupied a very significant portion of his time.

In order to coordinate the efforts of his compatriots Garnet tried to have a general meeting twice a year to talk about their experiences, hear each other's confessions, renew their vows and make plans for the future. Clearly, these meetings were fraught with danger: a single raid could wipe out the entire Jesuit community in England, but as Garnet wrote to his superior, 'We derive from these reunions immense benefit which abundantly compensates for the risk.'[2]

At this time some of these meetings were held at a moated manor house called Baddesley Clinton in Warwickshire which had been leased by the Vaux sisters, who had sheltered Garnet at Shoby on his arrival in England. This house still stands and is in the possession of the National Trust. Nicholas had spent the winter of 1589 constructing several places of concealment including a sizeable priest-hole, which Garnet described as 'a very safe refuge in a well-concealed cave.'[3] This cave, or rather tunnel, was originally the sewer outfall discharging into the moat. The tunnel is narrow at 0.5m wide and for most of its length is only 1.2m high, although sections of it are up to 1.8m high. It was originally designed to be just large enough for a man to go through its length for cleaning and maintenance. To aid this, there were loopholes at intervals along its route to provide light.

Nicholas began by building a new garderobe turret so that the sewage now had a different discharge point. He then blocked up the old discharge opening into the moat and built a 'plug' of bricks and stone 12m down the passage to produce an isolated section of tunnel forming the hide. Finally he closed up the loopholes and converted an existing garderobe downshaft next to the chapel into a concealed entrance. This hide was long enough to accommodate a number of men but had the drawbacks that, in parts, the roof was so low the occupants would have to stoop and, as its floor was only just above the waterline of the moat, it always had standing water in it. The photograph opposite shows it as it as it is today. The loophole on the left has been re-opened.

The Fathers met for the feast of the Assumption in mid-October 1591. There were about nine or ten Jesuits and some seminary priests as well as some laymen who were on the run. Shortly before the meeting began, a drunken pursuivant had appeared at the manor and demanded admission. He was kept waiting until compromising items were hidden, and when he was finally allowed in threatened to return 'bringing with him men to break down the doors and demolish the very walls of the house.' Garnet did not take him seriously as the man was well known to be a 'foul-mouthed man, who was in the habit of spending days on end snoring on taverns' and decided to proceed with the meeting. Nevertheless, the matter must have been on his mind because on the evening of the last day of the assembly, he had a premonition of disaster and warned everybody not to tarry without good reason. A number of the party when they heard this got on their horses immediately after dinner and rode off, leaving five Jesuits and two other priests. As

The priest-hole at Baddesley Clinton
(courtesy Enlightened Images)

well as Henry Garnet, the party included the senior priests Gerard, Southwell and Oldcorne.

At dawn the next day, the house was raided. We have two accounts of the raid: one from Gerard's *Autobiography* and one from Garnet who, in a long letter to his superior,[4] describes what he had been told by Anne Vaux who had confronted the pursuivants.

Gerard recalls his first awareness of the raid:

> Next morning, about five o'clock, [at first light – a couple of hours before sunrise] when Father Southwell was beginning Mass, and the others and myself were at meditation, I heard a bustle at the house door. Directly after I heard cries and oaths poured forth against the servant for refusing admittance. The fact was, that four Priest-hunters, or pursuivants as they are called, with drawn swords were trying to break down the door and force an entrance. The faithful servant withstood them, otherwise we should have been all made prisoners.
>
> But by this time Father Southwell had heard the uproar, and, guessing what it meant, had at once taken off his vestments and stripped the altar; while we strove to seek out everything belonging to us, so that there might be nothing found to betray the presence of a Priest. We did not even wish to leave boots and swords lying about, which would serve to show there had been many guests though none of them appeared. Hence many of us were anxious about our beds, which were still warm, and only covered, according to custom, previous to being made. Some, therefore, went and turned their beds, so that the colder part might deceive anybody who put his hand in to feel. Thus, while the enemy was shouting and bawling outside, and our servants were keeping the door, saying that the mistress of the house, a widow, had not yet got up, but that she was coming directly and would give them an answer, we profited by the delay to stow away ourselves and all our baggage in a cleverly-contrived hiding-place.[5]

In the house above, Anne Vaux was delaying the raiders as long as she could. Finally, she had to give them admittance. Gerard describes the scene as she later related it.

> At last these four leopards were let in. They raged about the house, looking everywhere, and prying into the darkest corners with

candles. They took four hours over the business; but failed in their search, and only brought out the forbearance of the Catholics in suffering, and their own spite and obstinacy in seeking. At last they took themselves off, after getting paid, forsooth, for their trouble. So pitiful is the lot of the Catholics, that those who come with a warrant to annoy them in this or in other way, have to be paid for so doing by the suffering party instead of by the authorities who send them, as though it were not enough to endure wrong, but they must also pay for their endurance of it. When they were gone, and were now some way off, so that there was no fear of their returning, as they sometimes do, a lady came and summoned out of the den, not one, but many Daniels. The hiding-place was underground, covered with water at the bottom, so that I was standing with my feet in water all the time.[6]

It seems that Nicholas was not one of those hiding. Gerard tells us there were five Jesuits, including himself; two seminary priests and 'two or three lay gentlemen'. It's unlikely that Nicholas, a servant, would have been described as a 'gentleman'. Most probably as he was not at that time known to the authorities, he simply mingled with the household staff.

Garnet's letter tells us first that Eleanor Brooksby, the elder sister and nominal mistress of the house, fled to a hiding place. 'She was somewhat timid and unable to face with calm the threatening grimaces of the officer's men,' he writes. It was left to Anne Vaux to confront the intruders. Anne, presumably in her nightgown at the time, stepped forward and claimed to be the mistress of the house. 'Does it seem right and proper that you should be admitted into a widow's house before either she or her maids or her children have risen?' she demanded.

After some discussion, which gave everybody time to take the steps Gerard describes, Anne finally allowed them entrance. She described the scene later to Garnet:

You should have seen them. Here was a searcher pounding the walls in unbelievable fury; there another shifting side-tables turning over beds. Yet, when any of them touched with their hand or foot the actual place where some sacred object was hidden, he paid not the slightest attention to the most obvious evidence of a contrivance made for concealing them ... One picked up in his hands a silver pyx used for carrying the most holy Eucharist. As though he had noticed nothing, he put it down at once. Under the very eyes of another there was lying a very valuable dalmatic [a vestment worn by a deacon]. Though the man had unfolded everything else he did not touch it.[7]

When they tired somewhat, Anne offered them breakfast, which gave the servants time to hide any remaining incriminating evidence. Afterwards, they resumed the search for some hours. Finally they gave up, but exacted twelve gold pieces from Anne. This was perfectly legal – a suspect was required to pay the expenses of a search.

Garnet gave Anne Vaux every praise.

The virgin always conducts these arguments with such skill and discretion that she certainly counteracts their persistence. For though she has all a maiden's modesty and even shyness, yet in God's cause and in protection of His servants, a *virgo* becomes a *virago*.[8]

That is, a virgin becomes a virago. In modern English, the latter word is used to denote a shrew, but the meaning has shifted and was then used of a strong or courageous woman.

Baddesley Clinton today

Earlier that year, Garnet had lost the use of his house in Finsbury Fields. He tells the story later in the same long letter in which he had described the raid on Baddesley Clinton.[9] A newly-arrived priest, ignoring or being ignorant of the rule not to visit in the daytime, was entering the lane that led to the house when by an astonishing chance a young man caught sight of him, ran up to his mother and shouted: 'See, there's a seminary priest! I saw him in Spain. His name is Father Richard.' 'Get the constable!' commanded his mother. The priest got no answer to his knocking and turned to leave. As he did so he encountered the constable. He tried to persuade the officer that the identification was wrong, but was not successful. The constable 'with a great press of followers whom he had collected in the neighbourhood knocked at the door.'

Again by a great coincidence, one of Garnet's servants, Hugh Sheldon, who was minding the house in the guise of the gardener, had returned by a different road. Hugh saw the crowd from the window and called out to know who the men were. They answered: 'The constable, in the Queen's name is ordering you to open the door.' 'Open the door to you, why, pray?' Hugh asked. 'We must examine the house, the man here whom we have just arrested as coming to it. There is no doubt he is a priest.' 'Off with you,' retorted Hugh. 'You merely imagine he is a priest because you want to cause my master trouble. In any case, you did not arrest him here: you are pretending he came from here. How am I to know you are not thieves and want to sack my house? I shall be blunt with you. I am not going to allow anyone in today. If you use force it will be at your own peril. I shall defend my master's house.'

With this respite, Hugh made haste to hide all incriminating matter, including all the massing stuff and Garnet's papers and correspondence. It probably all went into Nicholas' priest-hole in the cellar. Meanwhile the constable left his men to watch the house and went away to bring the Chief Justice of Middlesex, Richard Young.

On this worthy's appearance, Hugh became conciliatory. He spoke politely to Young saying:

If it had been your Worship who had come in the first instance, I should have opened the door at once in answer to your summons. I am well acquainted with your integrity and with the authority you

possess [but] in such a remote, almost uninhabited spot I had every
reason to fear robbery.

Young asked about the priest but Hugh answered (truthfully) that
he had not seen him as he had been out of the house. Perhaps he had
come to the wrong door? Young then entered and looked carefully
around. He found a letter which Hugh had overlooked in which
Garnet urged a man to convert to Catholicism. When challenged
with this, Hugh denied all knowledge of it and claimed that he
couldn't read. Young put it carefully into his tunic as this was
evidence that the house was inhabited by a Catholic priest. He went
down into the cellar where Nicholas' priest-hole had its entrance and
looked around. Ostensibly trying to help, Hugh poked around at a
pile of coal as if he was checking if there was a trap-door concealed
under it, and the dust he raised drove Young back upstairs again.
Hugh brushed his silk tunic and gave him a drink. Young then left
but stationed men to keep an eye on the house. Hugh now had
leisure to burn the papers and at a later time was able to evade the
watchers and escape from the house. The Finsbury Fields house was
now 'blown' and Garnet would have to move elsewhere, but the
efforts of two of Garnet's servants had avoided a much worse
outcome.

At about the time of the search at Baddesley Clinton, Gerard had
made his base at a manor house called Braddocks, or Broad Oaks, in
East Anglia, which was the home of a recusant named William
Wiseman. As a precaution, the servants were all replaced by
Catholics, but Wiseman made the mistake of trusting an old
retainer called John Frank, who was a Protestant, and who began to
send regular reports to the authorities. An early result of his efforts
was that there was a raid on Braddocks in the autumn of 1592. The
pursuivants tore down panelling and found an old Marian priest,
Richard Jackson, hiding behind a false wall. Gerard is thought to
have been visiting his family in Lancashire at the time, so fortunately was not taken. He was however concerned enough to arrange
with Henry Garnet that Nicholas would come to Braddocks that
Christmas and build at least two priest-holes.

One of the priest-holes is now lost, but the other in which Gerard
was to shelter can still be seen. The chapel at Braddocks was at the

Broad Oaks Manor today

top of the house – a typical position; as far from the main entrance as possible. In the room is a fireplace and Nicholas had excavated a hole down into the wall below the grate. He hacked out a large quantity of brickwork, to make a space which was about 2m long, 0.6m wide and 1.9m high: just large enough to take a man. The cavity formed extended down behind the wall of the room below, which was the main reception room; an impressive room with a high ceiling.

John Frank did not live at Braddocks, and Gerard was often absent on his missionary work so it seems to have been difficult for him to arrange a conclusive betrayal, but then in the spring of 1594 he saw his chance. It was Easter and Gerard could be expected to be present for some days.

On Easter Monday Gerard rose early for Mass when he suddenly heard the noise of galloping hooves. Immediately the house was encircled by a troop of men to cut off any possibility of escape. Gerard describes the dash for Nicholas' priest-hole.

Seeing what was going to happen, we had the doors kept fast. Meanwhile the ornaments were pulled off the altar, the hiding-places thrown open, my books and papers carried into them, and an effort was made to hide me and all my effects together. I wanted to get into a hiding-place near the dining-room, as well to be further from the chapel and the more suspicious part of the house, as because there was store of provisions there, to wit, a bottle of wine, and certain light but strengthening food, such as biscuit made to keep, &c. Moreover, I hoped to hear our enemies talk, wherein there might be something, perchance, which bore upon our interests. These reasons, then, moved me to choose that place, and, in sooth, it was very fit and safe for hiding in. But God so willed it, that the mistress of the house should in nowise agree. She would have me go into a place near the chapel, where the altar furniture could sooner be stowed with me. I yielded, though there was nothing there for me to eat in case the search should last long. I went in, then, after every-thing was safe that needed putting away.[10]

Gerard continues by describing the search itself. It is notable that here, three years later, the search is much more thorough than it was at Baddesley Clinton. The pursuivants don't rush around aimlessly banging on walls; rather they first take care to isolate the inhabi-tants of the house, then make a coordinated search including taking measurements and soundings and breaking into suspect spaces. In addition, they are prepared to spend significant amounts of time on the task; where Baddesley Clinton was over in four hours, this search took as many days.

The searchers broke down the door, and forcing their way in, spread through the house with great noise and racket. Their first step was to lock up the mistress of the house in her own room with her maids; and the Catholic servants they kept locked up in divers places in the same part of the house. They then took to themselves the whole house, which was of a good size, and made a thorough search in every part, not forgetting even to look under the tiles of the roof. The darkest corners they examined with the help of candles. Finding nothing whatever, they began to break down certain places that they suspected. They measured the walls with long rods, so that if they did not tally, they might pierce the part not accounted for. Thus they sounded the walls and all the boards, to find out and break into any hollow places that there might be.[11]

In the priest-hole at Braddocks

The picture above is taken from inside the priest-hole, peering up at the entrance hole. This is the view Gerard would have had.

After two days work, the raiders decided that Gerard must have escaped and took the mistress of the house, Mrs Wiseman, and the Catholic servants away to be questioned.* They left the non-Catholic servants, including John Frank. Frank had made a great show of resisting the invaders on their first appearance, so Mrs Wiseman trusted him and instructed him that when the pursuivants had left, he was to tell Gerard it was safe to leave his hiding place. Most fortunately, she was security-minded enough not to divulge the exact location of the hide, but rather told Frank to go into the dining room and call Gerard by name. Instead, he took this news to the authorities. Now, enheartened by the news that a priest was certainly present somewhere, they returned the next morning and renewed the search.

---

* Gerard's account says they were taken to London, but they could not have made the journey there and back in the time available. In his translation of the *Autobiography* Father Caraman suggests that they were in fact taken to a neighbouring house for temporary confinement.

Gerard continues his story:

They measured and sounded everywhere, much more carefully than before, especially in the chamber above mentioned, in order to find out some hollow place. But finding nothing whatever during the whole of the third day, they purposed on the morrow to strip off all the wainscot of that room. Meanwhile they set guards in all the rooms about, to watch all night lest I should escape. I heard from my hiding-place the pass-word which the captain of the band gave to his soldiers, and I might have got off by using it, were it not that they would have seen me issuing from my retreat: for there were two on guard in the chapel where I got into my hiding-place, and several also in the large wainscotted room which had been pointed out to them.

But mark the wonderful providence of God. Here was I in my hiding-place. The way I got into it was by taking up the floor, made of wood and bricks, under the fire-place. The place was so constructed that a fire could not be lit in it without damaging the house; though we made a point of keeping wood there, as if it were meant for a fire. Well, the men on the night-watch lit a fire in this very grate, and began chatting together close to it. Soon the bricks, which had not bricks but wood underneath them, got loose, and nearly fell out of their places, as the wood gave way. On noticing this and probing the bottom with a stick, they found that the bottom was made of wood; whereupon they remarked that this was something curious. I thought that they were going there and then to break open the place and enter; but they made up their minds at last to put off further examination till next day. Meanwhile, though nothing was further from my thoughts than any chance of escaping, I besought the Lord earnestly, that if it were for the glory of His Name, I might not be taken in that house, and so endanger my entertainers; nor in any other house, where others would share my disaster.[12]

Gerard must have felt it inevitable now that he would be taken the next day when the pursuivants had the opportunity to investigate the strange construction of the fireplace, and he fears for the fate of his host and hostess who would be jailed and very likely have their property confiscated if it could be shown that they had harboured a priest. Strangely, however – Gerard is convinced that it was divine providence – they ignore the matter. He continues his story:

Next morning, therefore, they renewed the search most carefully, everywhere except in the top chamber which served as a chapel, and in which the two watchmen had made a fire over my head, and had noticed the strange make of the grate. God had blotted out of their memory all remembrance of the thing. Nay, none of the searchers entered the place the whole day, though it was the one that was most open to suspicion, and if they had entered, they would have found me without any search; rather, I should say, they would have seen me, for the fire had burnt a great hole in my hiding-place, and had I not got a little out of the way, the hot embers would have fallen on me. The searchers, forgetting or not caring about this room, busied themselves in ransacking the rooms below, in one of which I was said to be. In fact, they found the other hiding-place to which I thought of going, as I mentioned before. It was not far off, so I could hear their shouts of joy when they first found it. But after joy comes grief; and so it was with them. The only thing that they found, was a goodly store of provision laid up. Hence they may have thought that this was the place that the mistress of the house meant; in fact, an answer might have been given from it to the call of a person in the room mentioned by her.

They stuck to their purpose, however, of stripping off all the wainscot of the other large room. So they set a man to work near the ceiling, close to the place where I was: for the lower part of the walls was covered with tapestry, not with wainscot. So they stripped off the wainscot all round, till they came again to the very place where I lay, and there they lost heart and gave up the search. My hiding-place was in a thick wall of the chimney, behind a finely laid and carved mantel-piece. They could not well take the carving down without risk of breaking it. Broken, however, it would have been, and that into a thousand pieces, had they any conception that I could be concealed behind it. But knowing that there were two flues, they did not think that there could be room enough there for a man. Nay, before this, on the second day of the search, they had gone into the room above, and tried the fire-place through which I had got into my hole. They then got into the chimney by a ladder to sound with their hammers. One said to another in my hearing, 'Might there not be a place here for a person to get down into the wall of the chimney below, by lifting up this hearth?' 'No,' answered one of the pursuivants, whose voice I knew, 'you could not get down that way into the chimney underneath, but there might easily be an entrance at the back of this chimney.' So saying, he gave the place a kick. I was afraid that he would hear the hollow sound of the hole where I was. But God, Who set bounds to the sea, said also to their dogged obstinacy, 'Thus far shalt thou go, and no further;' and He spared His sorely-stricken children, and gave them not up into their persecutors' hands, nor allowed utter ruin to light upon them for their great charity towards me.[13]

Finally, after four days the search was called off. They departed and released Mrs Wiseman and her servants. She rushed to free the priest, who had had nothing to eat but a few biscuits and a small jar of quince jelly which she had thrust into his hand as he was entering the hide.

As soon as the doors of the house were made fast, the mistress came to call me, another four-days-buried Lazarus, from what would have been my tomb had the search continued a little longer. For I was all wasted and weakened, as well with hunger, as with want of sleep, and with having to sit so long in such a narrow place. The mistress of the house, too, had eaten nothing whatever during the whole time, not only to share my distress, and to try on herself how long I could live without food, but chiefly to draw down the mercy of God on me, herself, and her family, by this fasting and prayer. Indeed, her face was so changed when I came out, that she seemed quite another woman, and I should not have known her but for her voice and her dress. After coming out, I was seen by the traitor, whose treachery was still unknown to us. He did nothing then, not even send after the searchers, as he knew that I meant to be off before they could be recalled.[14]

Gerard escaped on this occasion, but Frank's betrayal was still undetected and he was to do more mischief in the near future.

These were all narrow escapes, but even in these first few years of his service Nicholas' skill and ingenuity had time and again defeated determined searches and protected the Jesuit community he served.

PURSUIVANTS

Arrest

Following his narrow escape at Baddesley Clinton, Garnet's morale was low. The immense responsibility of being personally responsible for the survival of the Jesuit community in England was too much for him. Immediately after the search he wrote to ask that he could be replaced as Superior: 'There is nothing I could wish for more ... than to hand over the torch to someone more expert than myself,'[1] he writes. Whereas four years earlier he had begged the General to send as many priests as possible, as soon as possible, now he warns that 'It is not worth the risk of sending them unless they are anxious to rush headlong into peril or dire poverty ... conditions here are so unfavourable. If God does not intervene all things will reach the verge of ruin. There is no place that is safe.'[2]

The lull in persecution after the Armada had not lasted long. The Spanish were active again. In 1590 they landed a considerable force in Brittany and took the port of Blavet (now Port-Louis). Successful engagements against the French and English forces were followed by their seizing the major port of Brest in 1592. The Spanish now had a naval base just across the Channel and it was feared that they could re-equip another Armada with a much improved chance of success. Yet again, the authorities feared that Catholics might act as a 'fifth column' to aid the Spaniards and increased their vigilance.

A major setback to the cause occurred in June of 1592: Robert Southwell, long Garnet's companion and second-in-command, was arrested. So important was the capture of this veteran priest that the Queen's Secretary, Robert Cecil the Earl of Salisbury, took part in his interrogation. Garnet was devastated by this blow. 'Our very gentle dear companion has been captured by pirates, and now in a broken and battered ship we are sailing without a helmsman,'[3] he mourns.

Southwell was also considered worthy to rate the attentions of the chief pursuivant, Richard Topcliffe. Topcliffe can fairly be considered the torturers' torturer. He had actually got permission to build and use a rack in his own home near St Margaret's church-yard, in Westminster. The appreciation of his talents was universal. To John Gerard he was 'the cruellest tyrant of all England ... a man most infamous and hateful to all the realm for his bloody and butcherly mind'[4] and 'an old man, grown grey in wickedness.'[5] Henry Garnet adds that 'he boasts that he gets more pleasure from hunting down priests than he ever got from chasing wild animals or setting snares for birds,'[6] and that 'he had erected, as became him, instruments for every type of torture, so that he should lack no convenience for wreaking his vengeance on Catholics.'[7] Richard Verstegan, another Oxford man and a Catholic publisher, opines that '[his] inhuman cruelty is such that he does not omit any torture,'[8] and that he was 'a mercilesse monster.'[9] Topcliffe could laugh at such opinions. He had the complete confidence of the Queen and indeed seems to have been amazingly intimate with her. One of his victims, a Father Thomas Pormont, revealed at his trial in 1592 that the rackmaster had boasted to him (perhaps in a conversa-tional mood between torturings) that:

> he was so great and familiar with Her Majesty that he many times putteth his hands between her breasts and paps, and in her neck; that he had not only seen her legs and knees, but feeleth them with his hands above her knees; that he hath felt her belly, and said unto Her Majesty that she had the softest belly of any womankind.[10]

With such a patron, Topcliffe could do more or less what he pleased. Although holding no official rank, his field of operations seems to have been extremely wide. He planned raids; took part in them; tortured the prisoners; cross-examined at trials and even assisted at the executions. One story told is that he was making a very long speech at the hanging of a priest, when the condemned man tried to interrupt him. The hangman chided the priest, saying: 'Peace, and hear our maister speake.'[11] He could even ignore the Privy Council. As Garnet wrote to Richard Verstegan: 'He did not care for the Council, for that he had authority from Her Majesty ... and when he pleaseth, he may take her away from any company.'[12]

Having received his orders, Topcliffe got to work with a will. He wrote his initial report directly to the Queen:

> Most graceos sovereiyne —
> Having F. Robert Southwell (of my knowledge) ye Jhezuwt [Jesuit] in my stronge chamber in Westmr churche yearde, I have mayde him assewred for startinge or hurtinge of hym self, by puttinge upon his armes a pr of hande gyews [pair of hand-gyves – that is, shackles] & there & so can keepe hym eather from vewe or conferrence wth any.[13]

Robert Southwell

The inquisitors were aware that Southwell was second only to the Superior in the Jesuit hierarchy and familiar with the whole of the organisation and were determined to extract everything they could. Unfortunately for them and despite Topcliffe's best efforts, they could not get Southwell to utter a word.

In later years, Cecil described the inquisition to a friend:

> They boast about the heroes of antiquity, but we have a new torture which it is not possible for a man to bear. And yet I have seen Robert Southwell hanging by it, still as a tree-trunk and none able to drag one word from his mouth.[14]

Father Garnet seems to have suffered from depression – hardly surprising in the circumstances – and to have brooded on the sufferings of his friend and on the similar fate that certainly awaited him. Already in the first seven months of that year, seven priests together with three laymen that had sheltered them were executed. A month after his friend's capture he wrote dolefully: 'For me and for no other man, tortures are already prescribed. Death itself would indeed be a delight.'[15] He also mentions again to the Jesuit General that he would be happy to be replaced as Superior.

Garnet was always moving about as part of his duties, but in this period he seems to have travelled unceasingly. It was largely by keeping on the move and regularly changing his lodgings that he avoided capture. Some letters for this period are lost, but he seems to have been trying to cover almost the entire length and breadth of England. He certainly went in a south-westerly direction in the summer of 1592 and is likely to have gone well into the West Country. He returned to London in the autumn, then went far into the north that winter, reaching Durham and Northumberland near the border with Scotland. Then back once more to London, before setting out to survey East Anglia.

Nicholas would have been with him through all of this. We can imagine them in bad weather guiding their horses through the deep mud of the unmade roads, and huddling under their cloaks from the driving rain. They would find shelter in the network of recusant houses but would often have to stop at wayside inns, where they would have to have agreed a cover story to account for their travels and would have to be careful to watch their tongues at all times.

In the middle of all this, Garnet got a letter from Aquaviva refusing his request to resign as Superior. 'I have given much thought to the question of substituting in your place another who will have charge of all our affairs in England and direct our work there,' he wrote. 'It is a serious matter. Your Reverence has now had much practice and experience, and also has other qualities that are needed: you would seem by far the best equipped priest for the office.'[16]

At Easter 1594 they were once more back in London. John Gerard had just had his narrow escape under the fireplace at Braddocks, and was also in London at that time, having decided to leave his regular haunts to let things cool down and visit some friends in prison. He records that he turned to Nicholas Owen to arrange him some lodgings. This is a talent of Nicholas' that we have not previously seen, but Gerard praises his skill in making the arrangements and implies that it was a duty he often carried out, describing him as 'that excellent man, who was so experienced in transactions of this sort.'[17]

The arrangements were made, and while he waited for the lodgings to be prepared he and Nicholas stayed in the landlord's own house in Holborn. Gerard had left the address with the Wisemans because he wanted to send messages to and fro, but calamitously Mr Wiseman sent a letter by the traitor John Frank. Frank left Gerard at about 10 o'clock at night, and went straight to the authorities. Gerard and Nicholas retired for the night. As was usual in Tudor times, they would have shared the same bed. At midnight, when they had just fallen asleep, the house was raided.

Gerard describes the scene:

Little John and I were both awakened by the noise outside. I guessed what it was, and told John to hide the letter received that night in the ashes where the fire had been. No sooner had he done so and got into bed again, than the noise which we had heard before seemed to travel up to our room. Then some men began knocking at the chamber door, ready to break it in if it was not opened at once. There was no exit except by the door where our foes were; so I bade John get up and open the door. The room was at once filled with men 'armed with swords and staves' [Gerard quotes from Matthew's description of the arrest of Jesus], and many more stood outside, who were not able to enter. Among the rest stood two pursuivants, one of whom knew me well, so there was no chance of my passing unknown.

I got up and dressed, as I was bid. All my effects were searched, but without a single thing being found that could do harm to any man. My companion and I were then taken off to prison. By God's grace we did not feel distressed, nor did we show any token of fear.[18]

John Frank gave a deposition after the arrest, in which he names Nicholas as having been present at Braddocks, although he doesn't seem to have known his purpose there. The paragraph runs:

Item, he saith that Nicholas Owen, who was taken in bed with Mr Gerard the Jesuit, was at Mr Wiseman's house at Christmas was twelve months, and called by the name of Little John and Little Michael, and the cloak that he wore was Mr Wiseman's cloak a year past, and was of sad [dark-hued] green cloth with sleeves, caped with tawny velvet and little gold strips turning on the cape. And the said Owen was at Mr Emerson's at Felsted while Mrs Wiseman lay there.[19]

In another paragraph he gives us the name of the house* while taking further care to implicate his employer.

Item, he saith that the satin doublet and velvet hose which were found in Middleton's house at the apprehension of Mr Gerard were Mr Wiseman's, and the ruffs were Mrs Wiseman's.[21]

Gerard was initially taken not to prison, but to the pursuivant's own house and kept there for two days before interrogation. He speculates that was because they wanted to question Nicholas first.

---

* Father Caraman in his biography of Garnet states that the place of arrest was at a tailor's house in Golden Lane, also in Holborn.[20] This must be a mistake, partly because of the evidence of Frank's statement above, and partly because that house had been raided only the month before and it is inconceivable a veteran such as Gerard would have taken such a risk.

THE POULTRY COMPTER. (*From an Old Print.*)

The Poultry Compter

Meanwhile, Nicholas was taken to a prison in Cheapside called the Poultry Compter: a Compter or Counter being the name for a small prison under the control of a sheriff. Here he was to get his first experience of torture.

John Frank had also betrayed Gerard's servant Richard Fulwood, and Richard was also arrested and taken to the Poultry. There, according to Gerard, the examiners first tried coaxing and bribery, then when these didn't work they had recourse to threats and when those didn't work they turned to torture.

They were both hung up for three hours together, having their arms fixed into iron rings, and their bodies hanging in the air; a torture which causes frightful pain and intolerable extension of the sinews. It was all to no purpose; no disclosure could be wrested from them that was hurtful to others; no rewards could entice, no threats or punishments force them, to discover where I or any of ours had been harboured, or to name any of our acquaintance or abettors.[22]

The conditions in which they were housed were very bad. Henry Garnet called it 'a very evil prison and without comfort.'[23] Gerard goes into more detail regarding his own conditions:

> I was lodged in a garret where there was nothing but a bed, and no room to stand upright, except just where the bed was. There was one window always open, day and night, through which the foul air entered and the rain fell on to my bed. The room door was so low that I had to enter not on my feet but on my knees and even then I was forced to stoop.
>
> However, I reckoned this rather an advantage, inasmuch as it helped to keep out the stench (certainly no small one) that came from the privy.[24]*

We can be sure that Nicholas and Richard Fulwood, being of lesser rank than Gerard, would have got conditions no better, and most likely worse.

Nicholas languished in the Poultry for some time – it's not clear exactly how long – until some Catholic gentlemen raised a large sum of money to have him released. This was probably organised by Father Garnet, who would have missed his help. It seems strange to us that such a procedure was possible, but in those times civil prisons such as the Compters were run as a business by the Sheriff and his staff and were essentially a law unto themselves – parliamentary inspectors having no jurisdiction within the walls. Prisons even competed among themselves for the custody of the most lucrative detainees. Inmates were charged for everything necessary to survival and comfort: food, drink, clothes, bedding, medical attention and so on. A prisoner such as Nicholas who could not pay for his own keep was a drain on the Sheriff's resources. The authorities seem to have lost interest in him when he wouldn't talk, and

---

* The Poultry did not improve over the years. A century later, one writer records that on a visit to the prison 'the mixture of scents that arose from mundungus tobacco, foul sweaty toes, dirty shirts, the shit-tub, stinking breaths, and uncleanly carcases, poisoned our nostrils far worse than a Southwark ditch, a tanner's yard, or a tallow-chandler's melting-room.'[25]

fortunately Frank didn't know that he was so valuable to the Jesuits, so they would have assumed he was simply a servant of little importance.

On the other side, the Catholic gentlemen who raised the money were acting in their own self-interest. If a priest were found on their premises they were liable to arrest and might well face the death penalty. Also, they were liable for heavy fines and forfeiture of their estates. In the words of the *Act against Jesuits, Seminary priests and other such like disobedient persons*:

> Every person [that shall] receive, relieve, comfort, aid or maintain any such Jesuit, seminary priest or other such priest ... [shall] be adjudged a felon ... and suffer death, lose and forfeit as in case of high-treason.[26]

These men would have had other servants on their estates with the skills to construct priest-holes, but they wanted Nicholas because he was known to be so competent at his work and because he was discreet and now of proven faithfulness, even under torture.

Nicholas was now able to rejoin Garnet, who was still sunk in despair. Southwell was executed in February 1595; Gerard was facing an almost certain death sentence; other Jesuits had also been arrested and every Catholic prisoner that was taken was being tortured for more information. While describing Southwell's fate to his superior he writes resignedly: 'I do not see how I can escape the enemy's hands any longer.'[27]

It has been suggested by an eminent authority that Garnet attended executions to give what comfort he could to the condemned man.[28] However, I find nothing in his letters to suggest this. Even though he regularly describes the scenes, he gives no indication that he does so as an eye-witness: perhaps he found it too distressing.

For the Catholic cause in England, matters had reached a very low ebb.

TOWER OF LONDON

Escape from the Tower

After he had been in the Poultry for three months, Gerard's friends paid a bribe and had him moved to the Clink prison on the south bank of the Thames. This was much more comfortable and Gerard was able to talk to other Catholics, say Mass, receive the sacraments and send and receive letters.

He was to be kept there for three years and, coincidentally, within that time Nicholas' brother Henry was also imprisoned there. Henry had completed his apprenticeship under Joseph Barnes and was now a journeyman. He had been printing Catholic books and pamphlets and was committed to prison for this in November 1595.

Henry had no intention of letting imprisonment hinder his work, and somehow managed to get a press into his cell. Another (Protestant) printer complained to Parliament that '[he] got so bold at last that he contrived to bring his press in with him to the Clink prison and there printed Popish Books.'[1] The Clink does indeed seem to have been run with a very light touch and bribery could achieve a great deal in making things comfortable.

Nicholas, now free, came regularly to the prison to visit his brother and John Gerard, and also John Lillie, another of Garnet's servants, who had been captured and was in the cell next to Gerard. During this time Henry Garnet mentions Nicholas for the first time in one of his letters. He wrote to Aquaviva in 1596 that:

we maintain a number of necessary lay helpers, and among them a carpenter. Some time God willing he will join the Society; his singular faithfulness and skill make him most suited for its work. He had travelled almost the entire kingdom, and, without charge, has made for Catholic priests hiding places, where they can shelter from the fury of heretical searchers.[2]

Things seem to have gone well for some years, but then Gerard was betrayed by an apostate priest named William Atkinson who was also an inmate of the Clink. He told the prison authorities that he had witnessed Gerard giving Nicholas a packet of letters from Rome and Brussels to be passed on to Garnet and that Gerard frequently received letters from abroad. The officials were now aware that Gerard was in communication with the Jesuit Superior and resolved to torture all the details out of him. So it was that in April 1597, Gerard was committed to the Tower of London. There he was questioned about the identity of the man who carried the letters and about the whereabouts of Henry Garnet. When he refused to tell them anything, they produced a warrant for his torture and handed him over to the interrogators. Gerard describes the torture chamber as 'a place of immense extent, and in it were ranged divers sorts of racks, and other instruments of torture. Some of these they displayed before me, and told me I should have to taste them every one.'[3]

They suspended him by his wrists for hours at a time over several days. Whenever he fainted he would be taken down and revived, then hung up again. Eventually he fainted so thoroughly that 'they could not bring me to, and they thought I either was dead or soon would be.'[4] They hung him up again for a short time, but as they were not able to get him to say anything and as he was clearly approaching death, they finally gave up and let him be in his cell.

The Tower of London has several concentric rings of defence. The outer ring is the moat, which is fed from the Thames. Then there is the outer wall, fourteen metres high and three metres thick. Not far within that is the inner wall and within that are buildings, including William the Conqueror's White Tower which is a fortress in itself. Gerard was housed in a small tower built into the inner wall and known as the Salt Tower. He became aware that there was

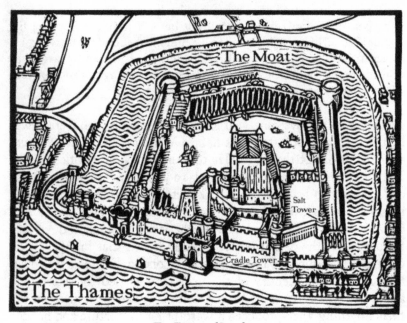

The Tower of London

another Catholic prisoner housed at no great distance. This gentleman, whose name was John Arden, was kept in another small tower, named the Cradle Tower, which in this case was built into the outer wall. Between John Gerard and this prisoner there was a small garden. The gentleman had access to the roof of his tower and was able to take his exercise there. The plan above will make the situation clear.

One matter that caused Gerard great distress was that in the Tower he was unable to carry out the duty of every priest to say Mass as he did not have the necessary articles. Then one day in July 1597, an idea came to him.

Arden's wife had permission to visit her husband and bring him a change of linen and other little comforts in a basket and as this had been going on for many years, the wardens no longer troubled to check the basket. Gerard had the thought that if he could only communicate with this man, the wife might bring in the massing items a few pieces at a time. However, he did not dare call to the man across the garden as it would be easily overheard. Therefore one day he attracted the man's attention while he was exercising on the roof and showed him pen and paper and mimed writing some words on it. Then he mimed holding the paper to the fire and then reading it. Finally he mimed the wrapping of a cross in the paper and sending it to him. Gerard's intention was to write his message in orange juice which would be invisible until held to a fire.

The next step was to bribe the gaoler to convey the items to the gentleman. The official made a show of being reluctant to do this, but in the end was convinced that it was very unlikely that the matter would come out and agreed to take the cross and a piece of paper on which Gerard had written a few conventional words on the other side to the invisible writing.

Anxiously, Gerard awaited Arden taking his exercise the next day. To his dismay he merely showed the cross and made signs of gratitude – he had not understood about the hidden message.

Gerard then decided to try again in more detail. He took an orange and showed it to the gentleman. Then he squeezed it into a cup. Then took a pen, dipped it in the cup and made a show of writing. Finally, he mimed holding the paper before the fire to make the writing visible. This time, the dumb show worked. The man read the letter and sent another back to say that it could be done if the gaoler would allow Gerard to visit him and that his wife would bring what was needed.

Bribing the gaoler to allow a visit was of course much more difficult than merely conveying a message or a small item which might be deniable. As the warder pointed out, Gerard might be seen crossing the garden or the Lieutenant might take it into his head to pay a visit. After much discussion and calming of his fears he agreed to the visit in return for the gift of a crown coin – more than a week's wages for him.

John Lillie had been released from the Clink and was visiting Gerard regularly in prison. Gerard asked him to supply Arden's wife what was needed, including a pyx containing a number of small Communion wafers. On the agreed day he went over to the gentleman's cell and was able to say Mass and Arden had the great consolation of being able to take Communion for the first time in ten years.

While Gerard was with the gentleman in his cell he noted that the Cradle Tower was built into the outer wall of the fortress, and from its roof one could look down onto the moat. He conceived the idea that it might be possible to toss a rope across the moat and descend from the roof of the building they were in to the other side. His companion gave the opinion that it could be done if a man had brave and resourceful friends. 'There is no want of such friends,' Gerard replied, 'if only the thing is feasible and worth while trying.'[5]

The next day Gerard sent a letter by John Lillie to Garnet to get permission for the attempt and Garnet wrote back with his agreement. It is certain that Garnet would have called a council of war to discuss the matter and that Nicholas as a 'practical' man would have taken a leading role in its planning.

It was arranged that John Lillie and Richard Fulwood, who had been Gerard's servant, but had now entered Henry Garnet's service, would come to the outer bank of the moat opposite the Cradle Tower. They were to wear a white paper or cloth on their chests so that they might be recognised as friends. Gerard would throw to them a lead ball attached to a stout thread. The rescuers would retrieve the ball and fasten a long rope to the string after which Gerard could pull up the rope make it fast at his end. They were to come by boat so that a quick escape might be made downriver.

A night was fixed, but Arden started to get cold feet and suggested that it might be better to offer a really large bribe to the warder to let them escape by a more conventional means. John Lillie was sent to him with authority to offer him a hundred pounds – perhaps ten years wages – and ten pounds a year for life. The warder refused this, saying that if he accepted he would have to live as a fugitive for life and would be hanged if caught. So it was agreed with many prayers to continue with the previous plan.

When the appointed night came, the gaoler was persuaded by the usual pleas and bribes to allow Gerard to spend the night in Arden's cell. Unfortunately, he not only locked the outer door, but also the inside door that led to the roof. The men had perforce to work at the stone into which the bolt shot with their knives until they were able to loosen it and allow the door to be opened. They then ascended to the roof, not daring to show a light or speak above a whisper because a sentry was stationed in the garden every night.

About midnight they saw the boat approaching with John Lillie,

Richard Fulwood and another man. They neared the shore, but just as they were about to land someone came out of a cottage nearby and seeing the boat make for the bank, hailed them, taking them for fishermen. He had no suspicions and soon returned to his bed, but the rescuers did not dare land until they were sure he had gone to sleep again.

They paddled about for so long however, that the time slipped away and they decided they couldn't accomplish anything that night. Accordingly, they abandoned the attempt and rowed away upstream towards London Bridge. At that time, the bridge was a very dangerous place for watermen. Because of the difficulties of construction it had been built with many short spans and this in turn meant that the river flowed fiercely through the arches. The drawing below was made fifty years before this date.

The Thames is a tidal river at London, and the incoming tide was flowing so strongly that their boat was captured by the current and forced against the piles placed by the bridge to break the force of the water, so that they could neither go on nor go back. The boat was rocked so violently, they feared it would be upset and yelled for help.

Old London Bridge

Gerard and Arden heard them shouting from the Tower and saw men coming out on the bank of the river with candles and getting into their boats to carry out a rescue. Many boats approached, but couldn't get close because of the force of the current. Gerard says that he recognised Richard Fulwood's cries even from that distance and 'groaned inwardly to think that such devoted men were in peril of their lives for my sake.'[6] Some men let down a basket from one of the houses which were built on the bridge, but Garnet's men couldn't reach it.

Very fortunately, a larger rowing boat manned by six sailors arrived and by vigorous effort was able to reach the craft in danger and take out Lillie and Fulwood. The third man fell into the river but was able to grasp a rope that had been let down from the bridge and was drawn up to safety. So all survived the night.

Gerard was cast down by this setback, but the next day John Lillie sent him a letter beginning:

> It was not the will of God that we should accomplish our desire last night; still He rescued us from a great danger, that we might succeed better the next time. What is put off is not cut off so we mean to come again to-night, with God's help.[7]

So once more they made their preparations. With some difficulty the gaoler was persuaded to let Gerard visit Arden another night and, by great good fortune, did not notice that the stone into which the bolt of the inner door shot had been loosened.

Gerard left three letters behind in the cell. The first was to the gaoler justifying himself for escaping and stating that he was being detained in the prison without having committed any crime. He says he did this so that the gaoler would not be blamed for the escape. The second letter was to the Lieutenant of the Tower in which he again exonerated the gaoler and mentioned the large bribe which he had been offered to allow his prisoners to escape and had turned down. The third letter was to the Privy Council assuring them that he would never meddle in affairs of State and only wanted to continue his mission of saving souls.

Once more with beating hearts they mounted to the roof. The boat arrived and this time got to shore with no disturbance. They found the lead ball and tied the string it carried to a rope. Gerard and Arden had great difficulty drawing up the rope because it was of considerable thickness and moreover had been doubled. This was on the orders of Garnet who had feared a single rope might break. Finally the rope was made fast to a stake on the bank at one end and wrapped around a cannon that was on the roof of the Cradle Tower at the other.

Gerard had hoped that they would be able to slide down the rope with little effort. This proved impossible however, because the distance was so great that the rope did not slope to any extent so they would have to haul themselves along it. John Arden who had earlier thought that the descent by the rope would not be difficult now saw it to be a very dangerous undertaking. However, he resolved to go on, remarking:

> I shall most certainly be hanged if I remain now, for we cannot throw the rope back without its falling into the water, and so betraying us both and our friends. I will therefore descend, please God, preferring to expose myself to danger with the hope of freedom, rather than to remain here with good certainty of being hanged.[8]

So he said a prayer and made his descent. He managed easily enough says Gerard as he was strong and vigorous and the rope was at that time taut. However, his weight had slackened it considerably which made Gerard's decent much more difficult.

Gerard then commended himself as he notes to God, Jesus, the Virgin, his Guardian Angel, his fellow Jesuits the martyred Robert Southwell and Henry Walpole and all the Saints and began his attempt.

> I took the rope in my right hand and held it also with my left arm; then I twisted my legs about it, to prevent falling, in such a way that the rope passed between my shins. I descended some three or four yards face downwards, when suddenly my body swung round by its own weight and hung under the rope. The shock was so great that I nearly lost my hold, for I was still but weak, especially in the hands and arms. In fact, with the rope so slack and my body hanging beneath it, I could hardly get on at all. At length, I made a shift to get on as far as the middle of the rope, and there I stuck, my breath and

my strength failing me, neither of which were very copious to begin with. After a little time, the Saints assisting me, and my good friends below drawing me to them by their prayers, I got on a little further and stuck again, thinking I should never be able to accomplish it. Yet I was loath to drop into the water as long as I could possibly hold on. After another rest, therefore, I summoned what remained of my strength, and helping myself with legs and arms as well as I could, I got as far as the wall on the other side of the moat. But my feet only touched the top of the wall, and my whole body hung horizontally, my head being no higher than my feet, so slack was the rope. In such a position, and exhausted as I was, it was hopeless to expect to get over the wall by my own unaided strength. So John Lilly got on to the wall somehow or other (for, as he afterwards asserted, he never knew how he got there), took hold of my feet, and by them pulled me to him, and got me over the wall on to the ground.[9]

After a restoring drink, Gerard managed to walk to the boat. They had hoped to retrieve the rope by pulling it from off the cannon it was wrapped around at the top end, but this proved impracticable. They therefore contented themselves with unfastening it from the stake and cutting off as much of it as they could reach so that it hung down the Tower wall and was less noticeable.

They rowed for some distance, then separated so that John Arden went with John Lillie to one safe house, while Gerard and Richard Fulwood went to a house Garnet had in Spitalfields. There he met with Nicholas Owen who had horses ready and a little before daylight they rode west for about 20km. to Garnet's country house, which was called Morecrofts* near the village of Uxbridge. They got there by dinner-time to great rejoicing.

Gerard was conscientious enough to care for his former gaoler's safety and sent a messenger to offer him a horse to make his own escape and to have a generous twenty pounds a year as a pension.

---

* Henry Foley in his work Records of the English Province of the Society of Jesus, published in 1877, says that their destination was probably White Webbs in Enfield Chase. This is not correct: White Webbs was not taken until 1600 and also we have the record of Father Tesimond who, on landing in England in 1597, reported to Henry Garnet and describes the house thus: 'It was about twelve or thirteen miles from London, near a village called Uxbridge, and the name of the house was Morecroftes.'[10]

He accepted the offer on the spot and was about to return to the Tower to settle matters and get his wife away, when a colleague met him and said 'Be off with you as quick as you can; for your prisoners have escaped from the little tower, and Master Lieutenant is looking for you everywhere. Woe to you if he finds you!'

The Lieutenant of the Tower, Sir John Peyton, when he could find neither his prisoners nor their gaoler wrote a report dated 5th October 1597 to the Privy Council:

> This night there are escaped two prisoners out of the Tower, viz., John Arden and John Garret [sic] ... The Manner of their escape was thus. The gaoler, one [Edward] Bonner, conveyed Garret into Arden's chamber when he brought up the keys, and out of Arden's chamber by a long rope tied over the ditch to a post they slid down upon the Tower wharf. This Bonner is also gone this morning at the opening of the gates ... I have sent hue and cry to Gravesend and to the Mayor of London for a search to be made in London and all the liberties.[11]

John Gerard had done what was universally thought to be impossible: escape from the Tower of London – the most notorious prison in England. Nicholas and his friends, with resource and courage, had worked together to achieve this near miracle.

Gerard's zeal and energy was inexhaustible and he got back to work at once. There were now four English Colleges established on the Continent and they were sending over an increased number of priests. Over the next seven years Gerard was to work with them to establish new centres to the north-east of London in Northamptonshire, Oxfordshire, Berkshire and Buckinghamshire.

During this time, he met Elizabeth Vaux, who was the sister-in-law of Eleanor and Anne and had recently been widowed. She offered to continue the family tradition of providing residences for priests and find a secluded property which could become a new base in one of the counties outside the capital. Gerard was delighted with this and, after getting Garnet's approval, they began house-hunting in Northamptonshire. They found a very large house, Kirby Hall,*

---

* Gerard does not name the house and at one time it was thought that it was the Manor House at Stoke Poges, Buckinghamshire. It is now known from the leases signed at the time that it was Kirby Hall.

in a secluded location and Elizabeth took a lease of it in April 1599. The next step was to get Nicholas to construct some priest-holes so it could be made safe in the event of a raid. Garnet lent Nicholas and Hugh Sheldon for the purpose and with Gerard they drove to the mansion where Gerard left them to make a survey.

The authorities had however guessed that something was afoot. It was common talk that Lady Vaux was about to move her household and the fact that a senior member of a famous recusant family was leasing a secluded mansion was bound to excite suspicion. Gerard and his companions were observed passing through Kettering, a nearby large town, and armed men were awaiting their return so that they could be arrested. Very fortunately, the road was bad and one of the servants suggested returning by a different route. They did this, and the pursuivants, on missing them, concluded that they must be staying overnight at the Hall.

The next day at dawn a large body of men arrived and attempted to surround the house. However Kirby Hall, which still stands, albeit in a partly ruined condition, is extremely large and they were unable to secure it completely. Nicholas was able to slip away into the woods, but Hugh Sheldon was arrested and taken to prison.

Kirby Hall today

As moving to Kirby Hall was now out of the question, Elizabeth Vaux elected to build a new three-storey wing at the family seat of Harrowden Hall. There can be no doubt that Nicholas would have been asked to devise suitable priest-holes in the new building and he would have been delighted by the assignment as he would have been able to design priest-holes in from the start rather than adapting an existing structure. A week after the Gunpowder Plot was foiled, Robert Cecil sent a party of a hundred men to search Harrowden, where Gerard had taken shelter. The search lasted a full nine days, after which they gave up. Gerard was hidden in a small priest-hole where, as he records, he 'could sit but not stand up.'[12] Sadly, Harrowden Hall was completely rebuilt after a fire in the eighteenth century and nothing of this remains.

Meanwhile, Garnet continued to move his base of operations as the pursuivants harassed him. His servant John Lillie was captured again in 1599 and during his examination William Wade, who handled many such interrogations on behalf of the Privy Council,* boasted that he knew of Garnet's town house in Spitalfields and intended to raid it within a few days. Wade gloated that 'I would never have told you this if I were not sure that you were a close prisoner and that you cannot possibly let Garnet know or anybody else.'[13] Somehow, however, Lillie managed to get a message to a friend and Garnet did not return to that house. He found a more distant property called White Webbs in Enfield Chase about 16 km. north of the City. White Webbs is long gone, but stood opposite the existing 'King and Tinker' pub which was built at about the same time and takes its name from a story about James I who took refreshment there while hunting. The Vaux sisters moved in yet again as housekeepers and Garnet was able to use this house as his London base for the next four years, at which time he began to fear for its security. There is no doubt that in these years Nicholas would have built several hiding places on the premises.

John Gerard was also changing his lodgings. He leased a house in London then, around 1603 together with two other priests, moved

---

* Tesimond, in telling this story, describes Wade as 'the Lieutenant of the Tower, a man of great cruelty towards Catholics but above measure hostile to our Society [the Jesuits]'. In fact Wade was not made Lieutenant until 1605.

to another 'nearer the principal street in London, called the Strand' which he described as having 'private entrances on both sides, and I had contrived in it some most excellent hiding-places.'[14] It is certain that Nicholas, who had always worked so closely with Gerard, constructed these hides. This safe-house was to play a weighty part in the history of England.

It is in this period that Nicholas took serious hurt. The strain of the very physical work he had to do had given him a hernia. Gerard mentioned this years later, saying: 'Now true it is, and well known to many, that the man had a rupture in his belly, taken with excessive pains in his former labours.'[15]

Gerard gives no date for this, but it is clearly a direct inguinal hernia which is most common in middle age when the abdominal muscles weaken and can no longer take the strain of lifting heavy weights. We can make a rough estimate of 1602, when Nicholas was forty.

Yet another misfortune befell him around this time. Gerard records that in 1599 Father Garnet sent Nicholas to London to fetch 'certain household stuff'. He loaded the horse in an inn yard, arranging the load behind the saddle. He then got into the saddle 'with great difficulty' says Gerard – he would have had to swing his leg over the load, a problem for one of his height, and he may have already suffered his hernia which would have made it painful. The horse:

> was somewhat resty [and] would not go forward, whether misliking his load or no, it is uncertain, but instead of going forward he rose so high with his forefeet that he fell backward and fell upon the man and burst his leg.[16]

Gerard says that he bore the pain with great patience. He had to stay at the inn, and when it became clear that the bone was not knitting properly, it had to be broken a second time and re-set. Gerard goes on to say that they all admired him at the inn for his patience and virtue and he was 'ever after most welcome to the place.'

After this misfortune one leg was a little bent and shorter than the other so from then on he walked with a slight limp. This charmed his Jesuit friends because it put them in mind of their founder, Ignatius of Loyola. Ignatius was once a soldier and when storming the fortress of Pamplona in 1521 his leg was broken by a cannonball, so he too limped for the rest of his life.

POWDER PLOT

The Gunpowder Plot

In 1603 Queen Elizabeth died and on her deathbed nominated James of Scotland as her successor. Catholics had great hopes of the new monarch. Although himself a Protestant, he was the son of Mary Queen of Scots, a fervent Catholic. Furthermore, he derived his right to the throne through Henry VII who had, of course, never been excommunicated by the Pope. Garnet was one of those who were hopeful and wrote to his superior: 'Great fears were: but all are turned into greatest security: and a golden time we have of unexpected freedom ... Great hope [there] is of toleration.'[1]

There were even rumours that Anne of Demark, James' queen, had converted to Catholicism in recent years, and certainly she refused Protestant Communion at her coronation. She did however have a reputation for being wayward and the Pope was later to remark that:

> Not considering the inconstancy of that Queen and the many changes she had made in religious matters, even if it might be true that she might be a Catholic, one should not take on oneself any judgement.[2]

In the declining days of Queen Elizabeth, a clandestine correspon-dence was carried out between the English and Scottish courts. Clandestine because it might well be though to be treason and not just bad taste to discuss how to govern the realm after her death. In one letter to Robert Cecil, the Queen's Secretary, James writes regarding Catholics:

James I

I would be sorry by the sword to diminish their number, but I would also be loth that, by so great connivance and oversight given unto them, their numbers should so increase in that land as by continual multiplication they might at least become masters.

But later in the same letter protests:

I am so far from any intention of persecution as I protest to God I reverence their Church as our mother Church, although clogged with many infirmities and corruptions, besides that I did ever hold persecution as one of the infallible notes of a false church.[3]

One might say here that James was almost arguing with himself, saying simultaneously that he didn't want to persecute the Church but at the same time didn't want it to grow in numbers.

On his accession, James made encouraging noises regarding Catholic toleration and moreover, putting his money where his mouth was, he remitted the £20 per month fines for non-attendance at church. Notes made by Sir Julius Caesar, Chancellor of the Exchequer, show that receipts from recusant fines and forfeitures dropped from over £10,000 in the last year of Elizabeth's reign to a little over £300 in the first year of James' rule: an enormous loss of revenue.[4] But then on the 9th February 1604, a little less than a year after his coronation, came a complete reversal of policy. James informed the Privy Council of his 'utter detestation of their superstitious religion.'[5] Three days later a proclamation was issued banishing all priests from the kingdom and not only were the recusancy fines re-introduced, but arrears were demanded.

It is not clear exactly why James switched to such an obdurate position, given that it seems that his personal wish would have been to allow Catholics at least some freedom of worship. The most probable explanation is that, during this first year of his reign, it had become evident to him that powerful interests would not accept toleration. In particular, the Puritans, whose numbers were fast-growing, had a profound hatred of many Catholic doctrines. On the other side, the Catholics had been so weakened and reduced in number by fines, seizure of property and long persecution that their support was of no particular advantage to him. Any hope that respect for his late mother would influence him was futile. A full twenty years earlier he had written to the Earl of Leicester saying 'How fond [foolish] and inconstant I were, if I should prefer my mother to the title [of King of England].'[6]

The hopes of Catholics having been raised so high, the disappointment was all the more bitter. As Gerard poetically expressed it:

What shall we think to have been the state of all Catholic minds when all these hopes did vanish away; and as a flash of lightning, giving for the time a pale light unto those that sit in darkness, doth afterwards leave them in more desolation?[7]

It was only a few months later, on the 20th May 1604, that the bitterness took practical expression. Robert Catesby, a member of an old and wealthy, although non-aristocratic, recusant family, called a meeting to outline his intentions. Catesby already had a record of disloyalty to the Crown. He had taken part in the Earl of Essex's rebellion against Elizabeth only three years earlier, and had only kept his life on payment of an enormous fine. Soon after that, he had organised a mission to Spain to urge an armed invasion of England on the death of the Queen, promising them Catholic support. No doubt mindful of what had happened on the last occasion that was attempted, the Spanish refused to commit them-selves. With him at the meeting were his cousin, Thomas Wintour; Wintour's friend Guy Fawkes and two other young Catholic men. There, Catesby outlined his scheme, which was to blow up the House of Lords at the State Opening of Parliament, so killing the King and the Crown Prince as well as many Lords and Bishops. After the meeting, it being Sunday, they heard Mass and took Communion. We know this from Guy Fawkes' confession that after taking an oath of secrecy 'in the same house they did receive the sacrament of Gerrard the Jesuit.'[8]

It is accepted by most authorities without question that this meeting was at the Duck and Drake inn, in St Clement's Lane, near the Strand.[9] On inspection, however, the evidence for this is not clear. Under interrogation, Thomas Wintour said that 'we met behind St Clement's'[10] and Guy Fawkes' statement agrees that they 'did meet at a house in the fields beyond St Clement's Inn.'[11] This seems to have been coupled with the fact that both Thomas Wintour and a later recruit, Ambrose Rookwood, were lodging 'at the sign of the Duck, in St Clement's parish'.[12]

Some consideration will show that it is unlikely that John Gerard would have agreed to say Mass in a semi-public place where a passer-by might have overheard the Latin liturgy, or even walked in, and where there were no hiding places. It is much more likely that they were meeting at the house he leased at the time which it will be recalled was in the same area, near the Strand. The conspirators said nothing of the Plot to Gerard, and after their capture the survivors consistently denied that he had any knowledge of it. Gerard himself in his translation of the *Narrative* describes it as 'this preposterous Plot of Powder.'[13]

It is remarkable how small the Catholic community seems to have been at this date, at least among the gentry. The same names crop up again and again and everybody seems to know everybody else. It

The conspirators in the Gunpowder Plot

will be recalled that Fawkes was a school-fellow of Edward Oldcorne, who had landed in England with Gerard.

We know little of Garnet's movements in this year. Only one letter, dated 29th January 1604, is in the archives, and that is brief and uninformative. We know from another source that he was in Lincolnshire at Easter[14] and that he was back at White Webbs at the end of the year. There is a priest-hole at Irnham Hall to the north of Peterborough, which will be described later in more detail, which is almost certainly Nicholas' work. Perhaps it was constructed on this journey. John Gerard also tells us that Garnet had begun to suspect that something was afoot, saying:

> Father Garnett . . . hearing [that Catesby] and other gentlemen of his forward humour did keep much together and had many secret meetings, he began to suspect they had something in hand that might tend to some commotion and that they did labour to get adherents for some attempt to be performed in a forcible manner.[15]

He says specifically that Garnet wrote to the Jesuit General on the 29th August 1604 seeking guidance. This letter seems to have been lost.

We come now to the fateful year of 1605. It started well for Father Garnet: he was in his twentieth year of service in the English mission and whereas on his landing only one Jesuit was at liberty, now there were forty-two.[16] In July he received a letter from his superior, who had heard from other sources that a conspiracy was afoot. This information had been passed to the Pope, who had ordered Aquaviva to write to Garnet in his name to do everything in his power to quash any such undertaking, which would be sure to bring ruin on the Catholic religion.[17] Garnet took this letter to Catesby and read him the Pope's directives; Catesby's reply was that 'what he meant to do, if the Pope knew, he would not hinder.'[18]

Towards the end of July, Garnet was visited by Oswald Tesimond, a Jesuit priest who had arrived on his apostolate seven years earlier. Catesby had told Tesimond the details of the Plot in confession and he urgently needed the advice of his superior. No priest may reveal what is said in confession, but Tesimond mentioned that his problem was in connection with 'some device of Mr Catesby' and Garnet replied that in that case Tesimond 'might tell it me with a safe conscience, because Mr Catesby had offered to tell me himself, and so it might be presumed that it should not be an injury to him or a breach of promise.'[19] Tesimond then agreed to pass on what had been told to him but insisted it be by way of confession since 'he was not master of other men's secrets.'[20] The two priests then walked together and Tesimond repeated what he had been told. Garnet was distraught: he now had confirmation that a plot was in hand, but as it had been revealed under the seal of the confessional he could do nothing.

Incredibly, Garnet's reaction to this information was to go on a pilgrimage. He was not in good health and he decided to visit St Winifred's Well in North Wales, a site famous for its miracles of healing. The Well had been a place of pilgrimage since at least 1115 and remained popular throughout the Persecution. Another reason for his wanting to leave London was that he suspected that White Webbs was 'blown' and didn't dare stay there more than a night or two. As he travelled, he gathered together a large party: there were the Vaux sisters; Eleanor's son and daughter-in-law; Sir Everard and Lady Digby and many others. In total, there were about thirty persons, including the servants, among which was Nicholas Owen.[21] The shrine over the well had been constructed a century earlier in the reign of Henry VII and would have looked much as it does today.

St Winifred's Well
(courtesy Leo Schwartz)

Presumably unknown to Garnet, Digby was himself involved in the Powder Plot. He had been asked by Catesby to rent a manor house called Coughton Court in Warwickshire and assemble a 'hunting party' of Catholic gentlemen. There is some debate as to how much of the Plot Digby actually knew, but it is not cheap to rent a mansion and he can hardly have doubted that there was to be some action against the Crown. It was clearly Catesby's intention that Digby would control the Midlands, while he was responsible for the London end.

On his return to the south in October 1605, only a month before the Plot was to be executed, Garnet went to stay with the Digbys at their home in Buckinghamshire and from there caught up on his correspondence. A little later, on the 29th October, together with the Vaux sisters, Lady Digby and her infant sons and Nicholas, he rode again northwards to Coughton Court. It's not at all clear why he did this: he was retracing his steps of a few weeks previously and furthermore heading for the Midlands centre of the Plot. Obviously, Lady Digby wanted to rejoin her husband but it was not necessary that Garnet accompany her. Some have suggested that he had to do this, as demurring might betray indirectly what he had heard under the seal of the confessional; but surely Garnet, as the Jesuit Superior, could have thought of a dozen reasons why his duties required him to be elsewhere?

In any event, they went to Coughton Court and there, on All Saints' Day, 1st November, he said Mass and preached a sermon on the text: *Auferte gentem perfidam, Credentium de finibus* – From the land of believers, take away the unbelieving people. This was of course later construed as a prayer for the success of the treason. Four days later, all London was talking about the dastardly Catholic plot to destroy the Houses of Parliament with gunpowder. Guy Fawkes had been arrested at the scene and his fellow conspirators were riding for their lives.

King James had lived with the fear of assassination all his life. When he was still in the womb, his mother, Mary Queen of Scots, saw her secretary Rizzio stabbed in front of her. When he was an infant, his father was strangled to death. When he was five, his grandfather was murdered and when he was sixteen, he himself was kidnapped. He believed with much truth that he was surrounded by those who desired his death. He was not a brave man off the hunting field: a courtier, Sir Anthony Weldon, once wrote that he was 'naturally of a timorous disposition' and that 'his doublets [were] quilted for stiletto proof.'[22] The Gunpowder Plot convinced him that the Catholic Church was his sworn enemy and he resolved to spare no efforts or expense to extirpate it completely.

It has been suggested that Nicholas was involved in the Plot. Philip Sidney in his book *A History of the Gunpowder Plot* makes the case thus:

It is probable, however, that he knew something about the Plot; for a man who was (more than any other in England) *au fait* with secrets affecting the Roman Catholic cause, and who was personally acquainted with all the conspirators, must have known pretty well what was going on. He was implicitly trusted by the Jesuit faction among the English Romanists, and it is quite likely that Catesby went to him for advice as to the best means of concealing the powder at Westminster, and arranging the train for the explosion. The operations of the conspirators beneath the Parliament House would have been thoroughly in keeping with the proceedings of one who had been for years past burrowing like a mole in scores of houses for the purpose of contriving hiding-places and secret passages. If, at any rate, Owen did not sympathise with the aims of the plotters, we may, nevertheless, reasonably suspect that he was acquainted with the details of the conspiracy.[23]

This cannot be true: it is clear from his letters that Garnet knew that only disaster for the Church could come from the enterprise, whether or not it succeeded, and Nicholas, as Garnet's servant and close companion for eighteen years, could not fail to be aware of his feelings on the matter and would never have become involved.

Soon after dawn the next day, Catesby's servant arrived at Coughton Court with a letter for Garnet. As he was reading it, Tesimond came in and asked what the news was. Garnet is said to have replied: 'they would have blown upp the Parliament Howse with powder, and they were discovered and wee utterly undone.'[24]

A short while later Lady Digby arrived and was told the news. In a letter from the Tower to Anne Vaux, Garnet recalls the scene: 'My Lady Digby came. What did she? Alas, what, but cry.'[25] She would have realised immediately that with the failure of the Plot, her husband's life was forfeit.

It seems that Henry Garnet remained at Coughton Court for almost a month. It's not clear why he stayed so long as Coughton would most certainly soon become a centre of suspicion and, as will be described later, the priest-holes there were not especially secure. Perhaps he was simply unmanned by the scale of the catastrophe. What seems to have persuaded him to leave was a message from Father Edward Oldcorne, who was still at the nearby Hindlip House where he had been stationed by Garnet seventeen years earlier. Oldcorne had heard that Garnet was at Coughton and 'in some distresse' and sent his servant George Chambers to invite him to Hindlip. In Oldcorne's later interrogation at the Tower he said that 'by his occasion he came thither about St Barbara day [4th December]* last ... and assured him that he should be welcome unto

---

* In Garnet's interrogation, he said that 'he came to Mr Abbingdon's house at Henlip by St Bartholomew's day, or a day before or after.'[26] This cannot be correct as St Bartholomew's day is the 24th August. Presumably stress caused a slip of the tongue.

Mr Abington and his wife, and as he hoped might remayne ther safe, and that his man George Chambers brought him and his man Nicholas Owen thither.'[27] Nicholas had visited Hindlip many times over the years and by this date it was riddled with the most ingenious hides he could devise. It may well be that he urged Garnet to accept the invitation.

So it was that Henry Garnet and Nicholas Owen left Coughton Court for Hindlip House.

JAMES

Capture

Hindlip House was a large and rambling structure, built on rising ground with a fine view over the surrounding countryside. The house that Nicholas knew no longer stands: it was burnt down in the early nineteenth century and completely rebuilt. Still, we have drawings of the old house and a romantic description from a book for Regency travellers:

> There is scarcely an apartment that has not secret ways of coming in or going out: some have back staircases concealed in the walls; others have places of retreat in their chimneys; some have trap doors; and all present a picture of gloom, insecurity, and suspicion.[1]

It was at that time the residence of Thomas Habington. He had converted to Catholicism in his teens and was one of the conspirators that attempted in 1586 to replace Elizabeth with Mary Queen of Scots. He served six years in the Tower for this, but was not executed, probably because he was Elizabeth's godson.

Garnet decided that this was a place of relative safety and elected to stay there for some time. He lived in a 'lower chamber descending from the dining room' with Nicholas to make his fire and attend to his needs. He took his meals with Habington and his wife, and with Father Oldcorne. The house would have been in a state of joyous excitement because only a month earlier on the 4th November, and after having been childless for her eleven years of marriage, Mrs Habington had produced an heir —William.

88

Hindlip House

In December Garnet wrote an open letter to the Privy Council protesting his innocence of 'the late most horrible attempt'[2] and denying that the conspirators had told him anything, much less sought his consent. The Council replied with a proclamation for the arrest of Garnet, Gerard and Tesimond; declaring all three accessories to the Plot and guilty of High Treason.

Edward Oldcorne had been chaplain in residence at Hindlip for seventeen years, almost since he landed in England with John Gerard, and had been assiduous in his duties; so much so that the house had become effectively a religious centre. Gerard tells us that 'his house might have been one of our residences in a Catholic country, such was the number of Catholics flocking there to the Sacraments, to hear his sermons, and to take advice in their doubts.'[3] Henry Garnet had had to assign him two other Jesuit priests to handle the work.

It could not be expected that activity on such a scale over so long a time could pass unnoticed by the authorities. Some years earlier, in 1596, the Privy Council had asked the Bishop of Worcester to investigate conditions in his area and he summarised his findings to Robert Cecil thus:

I have viewed the state of Worcester diocese, and find it, as may somewhat appear by the particulars here enclosed, for the quantity as dangerous as any place that I know. In that small circuit there are nine score recusants of note, besides retainers, wanderers, and secret lurkers, dispersed in forty several parishes, and six score and ten households.[4]

It needed only one person to weaken or be over-talkative for disaster to ensue and this happened in January 1606 when one of the peripheral figures in the Gunpowder Plot, Humphrey Lyttelton, together with two other conspirators, was captured. Faced with execution, he offered in return for his life to give information concerning the Jesuits and especially 'Mr Hall', which was the alias of Father Oldcorne. This was accepted and he told them that Oldcorne was at Hindlip House and he thought Garnet was there too. This betrayal of his friends did not advantage him, as they hanged him anyway.

The prospect of capturing the Jesuit Superior galvanised the government into swift action. Robert Cecil immediately sent a message to Sir Henry Bromley, a local Justice of the Peace, stressing the importance of the situation and requiring him to raid Hindlip.

Cecil's secretary, Levinus Munck, included with the instructions the most detailed advice on detecting priest-holes:

In the search, first observe the parlour where they use to dine and sup; in the last part of that parlour it is conceived there is some vault, which to discover, you must take care to draw down the wainscot, whereby the entry into the vault may be discovered. The lower parts of the house must be tried with a broach [rod], by putting the same into the ground some foot or two, to try whether there may be perceived some timber, which if there be, there must be some vault underneath it. For the upper rooms you must observe whether they be more in breadth than the lower rooms, and look in which places the rooms must be enlarged, by pulling out some boards you may discover some vaults. Also, if it appear that there be some corners to the chimneys, and the same boarded, if the boards be taken away there will appear some secret place. If the walls seem to be thick and covered with wainscot, being tried with a gimlet, if it strike not the wall but go through, some suspicion is to be had thereof. If there be any double loft, some two or three feet, one

Robert Cecil, Earl of Salisbury

above another, in such places any person may be harboured privately. Also, if there be a loft towards the roof of the house, in which there appears no entrance out of any other place or lodging, it must of necessity be opened and looked into, for these be ordinary places of hovering [hiding].[5]

We have a number of contemporary sources that include a description of the raid or aspects of it. The most important is known as the *Narrative of the Gunpowder Plot* or simply the *Narrative*. This is usually attributed to John Gerard because the manuscript written in English was discovered in his handwriting. On inspection, however, it is clear from phrases such as: 'I have heard Father Gerard protest' and: '[I have] heard from Father Gerard himself' that he was transcribing a work of another author. A parallel document is: *The Gunpowder Plot: The Narrative of Oswald Tesimond alias Greenway*. This was written in (bad) Italian by Tesimond and as it closely follows the Narrative was for many years thought to be a translation. It is now believed that both these works were derived from a now-lost report in Latin on the Gunpowder Plot prepared around 1607 by an English priest and sent to Rome.[6]

We have some indication as to the authorship of this report: one line that appears in both the English and Italian manuscripts is: 'I was hidden with six other priests, in a place prepared by Owen.'[7] This clearly refers to the adventure at Baddesley Clinton which Gerard describes in his Autobiography. Gerard lists his companions as four Jesuits and two seminary priests. He names the Jesuits, who by the date of writing are all dead or in exile, so the report must have been prepared by one of the seminary priests, whose names, unfortunately, we don't have. Occasionally the Gerard and Tesimond descriptions diverge, and in these cases it can be assumed that they are supplementing the original text from their own knowledge. Unless otherwise stated, references here to the Narrative have a parallel in the Italian version.

There is an interesting manuscript in the British Library entitled: 'A true discovery of the service performed at Henlip, the house of Mr Thomas Abbingdon, for the apprehension of Mr Henry Garnet, alias Wolley, provincial of the Jesuits, and other dangerous persons, there found in January last, 1605'.[8] It obviously draws on contemporary sources and forms a useful overview of the raid. We need not rely on it too much, however, because we have eye-witness accounts from Henry Bromley and from Garnet himself. The latter are of especial interest: while imprisoned in the Tower, Garnet wrote letters to Anne Vaux ostensibly concerning matters of little importance, but between the lines he wrote more information in orange juice. This trick had worked in the past for Gerard, but obviously the authorities had become wise to the ruse. The letters are in the Public Records Office in their original form including the passages written in orange juice. It must be, therefore, that the authorities intercepted the letters, read the contents, then had exact copies made, down to the orange-juice lines and sent them on their way to keep the correspondence going.*

---

* It is likely that the person executing the forgery was a man named Arthur Gregory who wrote to Cecil later that year describing his success in 'discovering the secret writing' and ability to 'write in another man's hand'.[9]

The *Narrative* describes the besetting of Hindlip:

> He came therefore to the house on a Sunday morning very early [in fact it was Monday, 20th January], accompanied with above a hundred men, armed with guns and all kinds of weapons, more fit for an army than an orderly search. And beginning to beat at the gate with great importunity to be instantly let in, the Catholics within the house soon perceiving their intentions, made all the haste possible to hide both the priests and the Church stuff and books, and all such persons and things as belonged to the priests or might give cause of suspicion. In the meantime, sending to the gates, as the custom is, to know the cause of their coming, and to keep them in talk with messages to and fro, from the master and mistress of the house, all to gain time, whilst they within were hiding all things in the most safe places they had.[10]

One can imagine the consternation within the house as everyone ran around throwing incriminating objects into hiding places. Nicholas and Father Oldcorne's servant, Ralph Ashley, were hurried into one priest-hole and Garnet and Oldcorne into another. The time must have been very short, because Nicholas and Ashley had only one apple between them. Garnet and Oldcorne were in a better case because Nicholas had installed a narrow tube from an adjoining bedroom into the hide. Down this, water and thin broth could be transferred to the occupants with minimal danger of detection.

Tesimond's account praises the security of Hindlip, saying:

> That house was among the safest that existed, not merely in the county but in the whole of England. It was a fine, large house and for that reason well suited to concealing secret places ... The occupants had had good experience of this in many searches. Not once in all of them had they ever been able to find a priest, although it was taken as almost certain that they were there all the time.[11]

Nicholas' work was about to be tested as never before.

Gerard's translation continues:

> But Sir Henry Bromley, impatient of this delay, caused the gates with great violence to be broken down, which yet he could not perform in

so short a time (by reason they were very strong and answerable to the greatness of the house) before they within had made all safe which they would hide from this violent invasion. The Knight being entered by force, sent presently some principal persons with men enough to assist each of them into all the several parts of the house, as well as to take possession of the same, as to seize any persons that were suspicious, and to be sure that nothing should then be hidden after his entry.[12]

Thomas Habington had been away from home for some weeks, so Sir Henry showed Mrs Habington his warrant and distributed his men to search the house with great thoroughness. Very quickly, they found that some beds were warm (presumably there hadn't been enough time to turn them) and that there were books and clothing lying around that spoke of sudden flight. Mr Habington returned on Monday evening and was also shown the warrant, but denied that there were any priests in his house. Nothing was found on that day or Tuesday, but on Wednesday they found some small hides that contained 'massing stuff' such as vestments and altar furnishings.

On the Thursday, Sir Henry was able to send a report to Robert Cecil. It began thus:

My especial good Lord, I have pursued the service your lordship and the rest of the Lords have imposed on me for the search of the traitors; and gave it for gone, for that I could never get from Mrs Abington or any other in the house the least glimmering of any of these traitors, or any other treason to be here. Some presumption I had (besides your lordship's commandment) to continue me here, as finding beds warm, and sundry parcels or apparel and books and writing, that showed some scholars used. Mr Abington was not at home when I came, but was gone to Pepperhill, to Mr Talbot's, and came home on Monday night. I showed him his majesty's proclamation and my warrant for the search; but he absolutely denieth that he knoweth or ever saw any of these parties but Gerard in his youth, some four or five and twenty years ago, and never saw him sithence. I did never hear so impudent liars as I find here – all recusants, and all resolved to confess nothing, what danger soever they incur. I, holding my resolution to keep watch longer (though I was out of all hope to find any man or any thing) yet at last, yesterday, Wednesday, found a number of Popish trash hid under boards in three or four several places.[13]

Edward Oldcorne

That morning, Nicholas Owen and Ralph Ashley had been taken. They had decided that they could not remain in their priest-hole any longer and in an act of desperation had tried to creep out and mingle with the rest of the household.

The *Narrative* describes the attempt:

They therefore perceiving that some of the searchers did continually by turns watch and walk up and down in the room where they were hidden, which was a long and fair gallery four square, going round about the house, they watched their time when the searchers were furthest off, and came out so secretly and stilly, and shut the place again so finely, that they were not one whit heard or perceived when or where they came out, and so they walked in the gallery towards the door, which they thought belike to have found open. But the searchers being turned back in their walk, and perceiving two strange men to be there, whom they had not seen before, presently ran unto them, and asked what they were. They answered they were men that were in the house, and would be content to depart if it pleased them. The others asked whether they were Priests: they answered they were Catholics, and that further they would not answer, being no doubt desirous to be taken for such, the better to satisfy the insatiable mind of those blood-suckers. Then being asked where they had been all that while, they answered they had hid themselves, being Catholics, to avoid taking. And being urged to tell or show the place where, they absolutely refused.[14]

So Nicholas Owen was captured by his enemies. It is clear that they tried to give their captors the impression that they were indeed the priests they were looking for, because Sir Henry's report to Cecil concludes:

So that this Thursday morning two are come forth for hunger and cold, that give themselves other names; but surely one of them, I trust, will prove Greenway, and I think the other be Hall. [Greenway and Hall were the aliases of Oswald Tesimond and Edward Oldcorne respectively; Sir Henry seems not to be aware that Garnet might be present.] I have yet presumption that there is one or two more in the house; wherefore I have resolved to continue the guard yet a day or two. I could by no means persuade the gentlewoman of the house to depart the house without I should have carried her, which I held uncivil, as being so nobly born; as I have and do undergo the greater difficulties thereby. I have sent you the examinations of the parties which I have committed, and do expect your lordship's pleasure what shall be done with them. More at large your lordship may hear either from the bearer, or from myself at my coming up. In the meantime, I trust his majesty and your lordships will accept of my willingness and readiness to do you better service when I shall be commanded. In the mean time, I most humbly take my leave of your lordship, remaining ever, at your lordship's command,
    Henry Bromley
    Hendlip, this 23d of January, very late[15]

This letter would have been despatched to London immediately. As the messenger was travelling on Privy Council business he would have been provided with a warrant to use the network of 'standing posts' originally set up by Henry VIII. Under this system, certain towns along main roads were required to keep constantly available fresh horses for the use of Royal messengers. It was laid down that post-horses should travel at a minimum speed of five miles per hour in the winter[16] and therefore the letter would have arrived in London within twenty hours of despatch.

It may be that the Gunpowder Plot conspirators imprisoned in the Tower got to hear the news. In any event there is a conversation recorded between Robert Wintour and Guy Fawkes on the 25th January in which Wintour says 'There is a priest taken in Stafford-shire; what he is I know not, but I heard he was a little man.'[17] This might well have been a reference to Nicholas as Sir Henry's letter identified him and Ralph Ashley as priests and although Hindlip is in Worcestershire rather than Staffordshire, the counties adjoin.

The author of the *Narrative* implies that the decision to come out was Nicholas', referring to 'one of the two especially, whose name was Nicholas Owen, abounding in discretion.'[18] We're not sure why Nicholas and Ralph took the chance. Sir Henry says in his letter that it was both hunger and cold (remember that it was January). The *Narrative* agrees that one reason was hunger as they were: 'almost starved to death' but a more important reason was self-sacrifice as:

> they thought it best to come out; and yet not that so much to save themselves from death by famine, as for that they perceived the resolution of the searchers to be of staying in the house until they had either found or famished those whom they knew to be within. Therefore these two virtuous men being in hope that upon their taking, the searchers would be satisfied and depart ... this hope made them resolve to offer themselves to their enemies' hands, to save the lives of those whom they loved better than themselves.[19]

Any or all of these reasons might be true, but I would add to them the ravages of thirst. We have many examples in modern times of prisoners on hunger-strike living for a month or more, and the near-certainty of the rack and execution would surely have strengthened the will of those concealed, but it is not possible to last for more than a few days without water.

Garnet believed that, on the contrary, the discovery of Nicholas and Ralph gave new impetus to the search and blamed them for his capture. In an intercepted letter to Anne Vaux after his arrest he wrote that 'we had escaped if the first two hidden soldiers had not come out so soon, for when they found them they were curious to find their place.'[20]

In the event, Sir Henry Bromley was not inclined to give up, and his men continued the search until on the eighth day, the 27th January, Father Garnet and Father Oldcorne were found in a priest-hole built into a chimney. The *True Discovery* manuscript gives us details of the multitude of hides that were encountered in the search, most or all of which would have been Nicholas' work, although apparently the pursuivants apparently never did locate Nicholas and Ralph's hide.

> proceeding on according to the trust reposed in him [Sir Henry] in the gallery over the gate there were found two cunning and very artificial conveyances in the main brick-wall, so ingeniously framed, and with such art, as it cost much labour ere they could be found. Three other secret places, contrived by no less skill and industry, were found in and about the chimneys, in one whereof two of the traitors were close concealed. . . . Eleven secret corners and conveyances were found in the said house, all of them having books, Massing stuff, and Popish trumpery in them, only two excepted, which appeared to have been found on former searches, and therefore had now the less credit given to them; but Mayster Abbingdon would take no knowledge of any of these places, nor that the books, or Massing stuff, were any of his, until at length the deeds of his lands being found in one of them, whose custody doubtless he would not commit to any place of neglect, or where he should have no intelligence of them, whereto he could [not] then devise any sufficient excuse.

The *True Discovery* later describes the moment of Bromley's triumph:

> Forth of this secret and most cunning conveyance came Henry Garnet, the Jesuit, sought for, and another with him, named Hall [Oldcorne]; marmalade and other sweetmeats were found there lying by them; but their better maintenance had been by a quill or reed, through a little hole in the chimney that backed another chimney into the gentlewoman's chamber; and by that passage caudles, broths, and warm drinks had been conveyed in unto them.

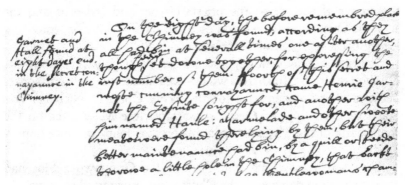

The True Discovery *manuscript describes the finding of the priests*

In his letter to Anne, Garnet gives his own description of the ordeal:

After we had been in the hoale seven days and seven nights and
some odd hours, every man may well think we were well wearyed,
and indeed so it was, for we generally satte, save that some times
we could half stretch ourselves, the place not being high eno', and
we had our legges so straitened that we could not, sitting, find
place for them, so that we both were in continuous paine of our
legges, and both our legges, especially mine, were much swollen
and mine continued so till I came to the Tower. If we had had but
one half-day's liberty to come forth, we had eased the place from
books and furniture, that having with us a close stool [a lidded box
containing a chamber pot] we could have abidden a quarter of a
year. For that all my friends will wonder at, especially in me, that
neither of us went to the stoole all the while, though we had means
to do *servitii piccoli* [urination] whereof also were at a nonplus the
day of our taking.

We were very merry and content within, and heard the searchers
every day most curious over us, which made me indeed think the
place would be found. When we came forth we appeared like ghosts.[21]

Bromley treated the priests well after capture. Garnet writes that he
and Oldcorne were taken to Bromley's own home at Holt Castle and
were allowed to spend several days recuperating. Garnet doesn't
record what happened to Owen and Ashley, but presumably being
servants they were taken to Worcester jail. In early February
Bromley assembled all his prisoners, including Thomas Habington,

the owner of the house; the priests Garnet and Oldcorne and the servants Owen and Ashley and escorted them to London, travelling slowly because of Garnet's weakness.

At London, they were separated. Henry Garnet was taken to the Gatehouse at Westminster which was used for state prisoners because of its convenience for the Privy Council. Nicholas was taken to the jail often used for recusants, the Marshalsea on the south bank of the Thames, where his brother John was once imprisoned.

The foolish men that had devised the Gunpowder Plot had caused yet more damage to the Church they purported to serve.

NICHOLAS OWEN

The Hides

Although we know that Nicholas built many hiding places in his eighteen years of service, there are only two priest-holes where we have documentary evidence that they are of his construction. Happily, both of these survive: one is at Braddocks and the other at Baddesley Clinton. In both cases John Gerard used the hide to shelter from his pursuers, and Nicholas' skill is acknowledged in his *Autobiography* and in both Gerard's and Tesimond's versions of the *Narrative*.

The first organised survey of priest-holes and other hides was published by Alan Fea in 1901 as *Secret Chambers and Hiding Places*. An updated and expanded survey was published by Granville Squiers in 1933 as *Secret Hiding Places*. An indefatigable worker who loved his romantic hobby, Squiers went all over the country, not only surveying hides that were already known, but seeking out ones that had been described in contemporary writings but had since been lost. His greatest triumph was at Braddocks (Broad Oaks Manor) in Essex, where, as will be recalled, John Gerard hid under a fireplace. In 1931 Squiers was allowed by the owner to make an inspection using Gerard's *Autobiography* as a guide. They found the fireplace in the old chapel at the top of the house blocked up, but opened it and cleared out generations of birds' nests that had accumulated there. They then lifted two or three layers of brick from the grate to find to their delight Gerard's hiding place still intact. Later, searching through the debris that had collected in the priest-hole, they discovered some tiny fragments of wood ash, which were very likely some of those that floated down upon Gerard as he cowered in his hiding place with the pursuivants making a fire above his head.[1]

Elsewhere in his book Squiers gives ample evidence of his energy and commitment, describing for example how he punted around the moat of a manor house looking for concealed entrances and how he spent a winter's day on the roof of Harvington Hall, putting a plumb line down the chimneys to see if any were false.

A modern and more rigorous treatment of the same subject is by the noted recusant scholar Michael Hodgetts, who published his own book, also called *Secret Hiding Places*, in 1989.

The author of the *Narrative* names Owen as the chief artificer of priest-holes. He writes:

> one Nicholas Owen, commonly called and most known by the name of Little John. By which name he was so famous and so much esteemed by all Catholics, especially those of the better sort, that few in England, either Priests or others, were of more credit. ... his chief employment was in making of secret places to hide Priests and Church stuff in from the fury of searches; in which kind he was so skilful both to devise and frame the places in the best manner, and his help therein desired in so many places, that I verily think no man can be said to have done more good of all those that laboured in the English vineyard. For, first, he was the immediate occasion of saving the lives of many hundreds of persons, both ecclesiastical and secular, and of the estates also of these seculars, which had been lost and forfeited many times over if the Priests had been taken in their houses; of which some have escaped, not once but many times, in several searches that have come to the same house, and sometimes five or six Priests together at the same time ... How many Priests then may we think this man did save by his endeavours in the space of seventeen years, having laboured in all shires and in the chiefest Catholic houses of England?[2]

It might seem that the writer exaggerates here when he speaks of 'many hundreds of persons'. As we have seen, more than one person might be secreted in a hide, and some hides might be used more than once; still some priest-holes would in the nature of things never be put to the test. The explanation is probably in his including the owners of the property where the priest was secreted and their families. If a discovery had been made they would also be liable to imprisonment and death. A reasonable guess would be that Nicholas built perhaps 150–200 hides of various sizes in the course of his career.

The appreciation continues with praise for his reticence: he worked on what we would now call a 'need to know' basis. The words are:

> One reason that made him so much desired by Catholics of account, who might have had other workmen enough to make conveyances in their houses, was a known and tried care he had of secrecy, not only from such as would of malice be inquisitive, but from all others to whom it belonged not to know; in which he was so careful that you should never hear him speak of any houses or places where he had made such hides, though sometimes he had occasion to discourse of the fashion of them for the making of others.[3]

We are also told that he always took Communion the day he started work and that 'as much as his labour would give him leave, did continually pray whilst he was working.'[4]

There is some question as to whether Nicholas worked alone. Oswald Tesimond tells us that he normally did, saying: 'He usually worked alone. In this way, it was easier to keep his labours secret.'[5] However, when Gerard made a journey to Kirby Hall to arrange the construction of priest-holes before moving in, he records that 'we left Little John behind and Hugh Sheldon also to help him.'[6] Therefore it's clear that Nicholas did have help on some occasions. On the other hand Gerard is writing this in 1599, the year Nicholas broke his leg and about the time he suffered a hernia, which would have prevented him from lifting heavy weights. It seems then that he worked alone where he possibly could, but had to accept help for the heavier jobs, especially later in life as his body weakened. Certainly, Nicholas himself would have been anxious to restrict these secrets to as few persons as possible: he knew only too well how the rack could encourage loquaciousness.

One problem Nicholas faced would have been how to keep the purpose of his inevitably noisy and messy business concealed from the servants. As we have seen from Frank's betrayal at Braddocks, no-one outside the immediate family could be completely trusted. It would therefore be necessary either for the house to be empty or for there to be another job which formed the ostensible reason for the building work. At Braddocks, there is an ornate fireplace in the room directly below the priest-hole which is clearly of a much later date than the construction of the house. Squiers speculates that the installation of this gave Nicholas cover for his real work. Similarly, at Baddesley Clinton, the construction of the new garderobe turret could have been done in parallel with the conversion of the old sewage tunnel into a priest-hole. No doubt in many cases the owner of the house would invent some improvement or repair to give a reason for Nicholas' activity.

Squiers maintains that he worked into the early hours of the morning, saying: 'He would work through the small hours and be back in his bed before dawn ... before he started on the obvious work that formed a pretext for his presence in the house.'[7] But this is unlikely: building work is noisy enough at the best of times and in the silence of the night would have been clearly audible even in a large house, making it quite evident that some surreptitious business was in hand.

Nicholas was the chief, but not the only, constructor of priest-holes at the time. In the far north of England, which Garnet seldom reached, there was Father Richard Holtby, whom Squiers calls the 'Nicholas Owen of the North'. Holtby was a very competent and hard-working priest to whom Garnet had given the northern counties as his territory. He would have been the obvious choice for Jesuit Superior if Acquaviva had agreed to Garnet's request to be replaced.[8] Holtby was a very good, although self-taught, carpenter and mason. One of his hides can still be seen at Hardwick Hall, in County Durham (now a hotel). Holtby doubled the size of a brick chimney breast so skilfully that no join can be detected, and constructed a camouflaged door into it. There is no doubt that at the bi-annual meetings of the Jesuits, he and Nicholas would have spent much time in technical discussions and exchanging tips.

Catholic families might also ask a trusted servant with the requisite skills to build hides. A spy reported on one recusant as follows:

Mr Bentley hath an old man named Green, a carpenter and mason, who ... made a secret place in Mr Bentley's house at Lea with a door

of freestone that no man could ever judge there were any such place
and makes all the secret places in that county.[9]

We can't talk about Nicholas' 'style' of construction as we would for
a conventional designer because he was careful not to have one. Any
sort of signature construction method would give aid to the enemies
of his faith. As the *Narrative* says:

> Yea, he did much strive to make them of several fashions in several
> places, that one being taken might give no light to the discovery of
> another.[10]

However, it is true to say that he had a certain fondness for excavat-
ing cavities within walls. An excavated hole had the great advantage
that no amount of measurement would reveal it. This was facilitated
by Tudor walls being immensely thick: even interior walls could be
two metres thick or more. The only problem was how to conceal the
entrance and here Nicholas would vary his technique. At Braddocks,
as we have seen, he made a cut down into the grate of a fireplace
and made a (rather crude) capping to hide the entrance.

There is another excavated priest-hole at Sawston Hall nearby,
which is regarded as one of the finest examples of concealment in
the country. Here Nicholas pulled up some floorboards at the top of
a spiral staircase and so exposed a corner of a very thick interior
wall. He cut downwards and inwards until he had enough room to
excavate a hole about 0.6m wide, 1.6m along the length of the wall
and 1.3m high. In total, almost two cubic metres of stone was
removed. This wall was made of 'clunch' a soft limestone which is
not suitable for exterior use but is easily worked and was often
favoured for interior walls. As finishing touches, a latrine was
chiselled into the stone at one end and a discreet slot was cut into
the outer wall to give ventilation from the courtyard. The floorboards were joined as a panel which then fitted very precisely back
into their original positions – Nicholas' joinery skills are evident
here. The staircase has no soffit, so the floorboards are visible from
below as one climbs the steps, and it is not at all obvious that the
curve of the wall gives just enough space for the entrance to be
chiselled.

The Stair Hide at Sawston Hall

Some distance away, but still in East Anglia, is Oxburgh Hall, a magnificent moated manor house built in the fifteenth century. The gateway arch is flanked by a pair of high octagonal towers. Inside, there is a bedroom over the arch. In one corner of the bedroom is a door to an octagonal room within one of the towers, then from that is a door to another room which has a tiled floor. By now one has gone through so many angles that it's not clear where this room is in relation to the outside. In the far corner of the last room is a recess, which Squiers speculates might once have held a small altar or a *prie-dieu*. Here, Nicholas burrowed down, then into the wall for about a metre, then upwards to excavate a large cavity within the wall. This is a palace among priest-holes and represents a high point in Nicholas' work. The maximum height is over 2.5 metres, the width within the thickness of the wall is 0.9 metres and the length about 1.3 metres. It is therefore in no way cramped and the occupant could even take a step or two of exercise.

Priest hole at Oxburgh Hall

It is fitted with a wooden seat, and behind it repairs to the plaster show that there was once a tube into the main bedroom over the arch. We saw this device at Hindlip where Garnet and Oldcorne were kept well nourished by drinks and thin broths supplied by this means. There are various small recesses for books and other items and on the opposite side to the entrance is another cavity about 0.6m wide, 0.9m high and 0.9m deep. This extension is under a small stair on the far side of the wall. The cavity is too small for comfortable occupancy, but could have been used for storage of bulky vestments and other Church stuff.

Finally, to cover the entrance, Nicholas constructed a pivoting cover made of a 200mm thickness of oak and faced with tiles to match the rest of the floor.

It would be possible to hold out almost indefinitely in such a hide. Oxburgh Hall is now owned by the National Trust and the priest-hole can still be visited and entered.

Outside East Anglia excavated hides are relatively rare for some reason. However, there is one at Billesley Manor (now a hotel) near Stratford. Here the cavity has been excavated quite high up inside a chimney breast, above the fireplace itself. Access is through the roof of a nearby cupboard which is built into the wall. The fugitive would climb up through a roof panel then through a crawlspace to the hide.

Nothing is known of the family that lived at Billesley, although the very presence of a priest-hole shows that they must have been recusants. Interestingly, the birthplace of Mary Arden, Shakespeare's mother, is only 2 km. along the road. The Ardens were a famous Warwickshire recusant family and as the houses are so close, and they were co-religionists, it is likely there was much socialising among the gentry. There is a local story that Shakespeare himself used the library at Billesley. Of course, such stories are ten-a-penny in the Stratford area, but given the circumstances here it is possibly true, despite the fact that Mary married a tradesman. Sadly, recent improvements and repairs at the hotel have resulted in access to the hide being lost.

One final example of an excavated priest-hole can be given, because of its unusual positioning and the fascinating story attached to it, although the hide itself is now lost and probably demolished. The site is at Scotney Castle in Kent. It has a most picturesque setting on an island in the valley of the river Bewl. The 'Old Castle' with which we are concerned was built in the four-teenth century and is connected to the mainland via a bridge.

The castle was the home of the recusant Darell family and the Jesuit Father Richard Blount was assigned to it by Garnet from 1591 as the base for his missionary activities in the area. In the dead of night just before Christmas, 1598, the pursuivants raided Scotney. Father Blount was awakened by the noise and just had time to pull on his breeches and grab some Church stuff and with his servant,

Scotney Old Castle

Bray, got into 'a secret place, digged in a thick stone wall.' The door of this priest-hole had been formed by pulling out one of the larger stones in an exterior wall and fitting it with hinges. Beyond the stone, a cavity had been excavated in the thickness of the wall, which must have been at least two metres square to take both men. The searchers spent ten days over their task. The sufferings of Father Blount and Bray can only be imagined. It was the dead of winter and they had for clothing only their breeches and a priest's cassock. For sustenance they had a bottle of wine and a single loaf of bread.

Mrs Darell had been shut up in one room with her children for the duration of the search, but at the end of that time she was allowed a little liberty as she thought. In fact, the pursuivants were watching her closely to see if she would try to bring food and drink to the priests they believed were hiding somewhere. Mrs Darell walked into the courtyard where the door to the hide was, and to her horror saw that the end of a vestment girdle was hanging out through the stone. She stooped and cut off as much as she could, but some still remained visible, so she called: 'Pull in the string,' which they did, but: 'Those that, it seems, watched her came presently to her and asked to whom she spake, and of what string.' She told them that she had called to someone indoors to pull on a string that lifted the latch so she could enter, but they weren't satisfied with that reply and began to search around the courtyard:

> beating with a beetle [heavy mallet] upon the stones; and many times on the door of the place, which was a stone in show not differing from the rest. With many great blows, the hinges of the door began to yield, at which they within set their backs to the door to support it against the blows what they could, but it was so much moved as that they saw the candlelight of the searchers and could hear all they said.

It grew dark and it began to rain very heavily and the pursuivants grew discouraged and decided to leave off until morning. They went into the Great Hall, built a big fire and sat there drying themselves, drinking and talking.

Father Blount and Bray decided that their best chance was to make a break for it, trusting that the dark and stormy night would shield them. Barefoot, they climbed two walls about ten feet high and got to the banks of the lake. It was eighty feet to the far shore at that point, and the water was covered with thin ice. Bray couldn't swim, but Father Blount thought that he could tow him over. Once he had leaped in, however, it was so cold that he realised this was impossible and called back to Bray that he would have to find another way out and meet him at a certain house, about half a mile away. Then he swam over the lake.

Bray decided to brazen it out. He burst into the hall, where the men sat drinking and called: 'My master has heard a noise in the stable, and says he thinks somebody is stealing his horses, and you all sit drinking here and nobody looks to his horses.' All he had on was his breeches and a priest's cassock trussed about him, but in the excitement nobody took particular notice of this and they all rushed out to the stables, Bray with them. When they got there, he slipped out of a door that led to another part of the lake where he was able to wade over. There, he met Father Blount who was stumbling about, having lost his way. Together they made their way to the house where a Catholic servant of Mr Darell lived, and got shoes and clothes. Their bare feet of course were full of thorns and badly cut. As the house was so close to the castle, they didn't dare spend the rest of the night there and walked on another fourteen miles in the darkness to safety. We have this story from a manuscript left by William Darell, one of the children who was locked into a room with his mother.[11]

The style and ingenuity of this hide make it likely that it is the work of Nicholas Owen. The argument against this is that there is no record of Garnet going so deep into the county of Kent. Then as now, the ports of Dover and Folkestone were the main entry points from the Continent and all roads leading from them were closely watched. Strangers could expect to be stopped and questioned at every town and village. We must ask therefore, how did Nicholas get to the castle? One possible explanation is that he travelled with Garnet's friend and companion, Robert Southwell. Southwell was of a much more dashing and reckless character than Garnet. He was a noted poet and his Nativity poem *The Burning Babe* is still often anthologised. His way around the difficulty of travelling was to recruit a few young noblemen to accompany him. This 'hiding in plain sight' disarmed all suspicion and he could go wherever he wanted. As he once wrote to the Jesuit General in Rome:

> I have sometimes called on the Protestant sheriffs to look after secret Catholics in their households; and they, seeing my fine clothes and bevy of aristocratic youths and suspecting nothing as little as the reality, have received me with imposing ceremony and truly sumptuous banquets.[12]

We know that Southwell often travelled into the south-east where he had relatives and connections. In the years before he was captured he tended to take turns with Garnet, so one would be in London while the other was on the road. There is a good possibility that Nicholas had been 'lent' to Southwell, as he regularly was to Gerard, on at least one of these occasions.

Apart from excavated priest-holes, there are many other types, based on creating or concealing existing voids. A variety of these can be admired at Harvington Hall, in Worcestershire, now in the possession of the Catholic Archdiocese of Birmingham and open to the public. This manor house has the finest collection of hides surviving in Britain, having no fewer than eight hiding places of various types.

The three most ingenious ones, which all use different methods, are grouped around the Great Staircase. This cannot be the original staircase, as it uses the 'open-well' system which was introduced long after the Hall was built. Hodgetts dates it at 1600–05[13] which would be when Nicholas had acquired considerable skills. It is likely that the installation of the staircase gave the requisite 'cover' for Nicholas' building efforts.

At the top of the staircase, there are five steps to a higher level. Two of these steps, complete with the riser joining them, can be hinged up as one to reveal a small hide, just big enough to take a man and with the underside of the stairs forming a sloping ceiling.

But this is not the end of the matter: the rear wall of this hide is made up of panels of brickwork separated by timbers. Today, the middle panel is missing but it can be seen from the remains of hinges and a bolt that once there was a secret door, faced with brick shims or otherwise camouflaged. Through this panel one can climb down into a spacious priest-hole about 1.5m by 1.8m and 1.8m high. The space for this was gained in part by inserting a false ceiling in the room below. This 'hide within a hide' is very secure in all ways.

Quite as good in its own way, is a hide opening off a small room known as 'Dr. Dodd's Library' on the other side of the Great Staircase from the hide above. On one wall is a massive vertical beam, fully 0.25m wide and running the whole height of the room. It has all the appearance of a structural member, but in fact it is pivoted near the top and can be swung out from the wall. It is then just possible to squeeze into a hide beyond. The priest-hole itself is reasonably big, being 0.9m wide, 2.4m long and 1.5m high. The beam could be bolted from the inside, so preventing accidental discovery. In this part of the house there are different levels and right-angled bends in an adjacent passage, so making the geometry very complicated and impeding the detection of the hide by measurement.

The Stair Hide at Harvington Hall

The Swinging-Beam hide at Harvington Hall

Interestingly, we have a description of a similar scheme at Grosmont Priory in north-east Yorkshire, which was the headquarters of Father Holtby. A pursuivant's report of 1599 describes a priest hole as being:

> at a stair head within a thick stone wall ... covered with a great post of the bigness of a man's body, which seemed to bear the house but indeed did hinge only and was removable to and fro.[14]

Holtby almost certainly learnt this trick from Nicholas.

In a nearby room at Harvington, again adjacent to the Great Staircase, can be seen a brick fireplace which has been built into a corner so that it is triangular in plan. This looks unexceptional, but closer inspection will show that there is no chimney breast on the floor below, so that the whole weight of the fireplace is resting on the floor beams. In fact, this fireplace forms a bolthole into the attic. A conveniently-projecting brick at the back gives a foothold and a fugitive can climb up into the garret space above. This is therefore an emergency exit rather than a hide. It should be noticed that the back of the hearth is convincingly blackened. As a fire could never have been lit here, this must have been done with a candle or something similar.

Once in the garret, the escaping priest would make for the north end of the block. There, two rafters have been cut away to allow entrance into a crawlspace running almost the entire length of the roof beam. At the opposite end, he could drop down into a very large priest hole, about 5m by 4m and 2m high at the apex of the roof. A hide of this size could easily take twenty people and is the second largest surviving priest-hole in the country (the largest is at Towneley Hall in Lancashire). This hide cannot be said to be particularly secure, despite the fact that the entrance to it is well concealed. Levinus Munck's directions to searchers will be remembered:

> If there be a loft towards the roof of the house, in which there appears no entrance out of any other place or lodging, it must of necessity be opened and looked into.[15]

Admittedly, the loft area is large and confusing but a hide of this size would hardly withstand a systematic search.

The four hiding places above are considered the best, but there are four others of less complexity which may be Nicholas' early work. One priest-hole has been formed by building a sandstone interior wall to create a small hide next to a chimney breast. The void created is rather small at 0.6m wide and 1.3m long but is the full height of the room from which it was divided. The entrance is through a trapdoor on the floor above; a ladder being provided to climb down. This hide seems reasonably secure, because the thickness of the sandstone would defeat a sounding-hammer.

At the opposite end of the house is another rather cramped priest-hole, being 0.8m by 1.1m in plan and 1.5m high. It is built into the interstices of a bread-oven and has an entrance formed of three layers of oak planks to deaden sound. The planks run the entire length of the recess in which the trapdoor is constructed, so that there is no break in the flooring.

The two other hides will be mentioned for completeness, although they are rather rudimentary and may well not be of Nicholas' construction. One is a small recess under the floorboards of a chapel. This is only 0.18 metres deep and could only have accommo-dated a single set of vestments for the priest. The other is a boarded-off area in a garret forming a triangle 1m wide and 1m high and being 2.4m long. This could just have accommodated a human, but was more probably used to conceal books or massing stuff.

We saw above an example of a 'hide within a hide'. There are others, although none quite so ingenious. An important one is at Coughton Court, where Garnet and Nicholas first heard of the failure of the Gunpowder Plot.

The gateway of Coughton is flanked by two hexagonal towers. The old secret chapel was located in an upper room of one of these towers, and off this room is a small closet, the original use of which is debatable. There was once a trapdoor in this closet concealing a double hide descending for over three metres down the length of the tower. The cross-section is about 1.2m square and it was divided by a false floor 1.2m down. We have lost the original false floor, but it must once been possible to lift it or part of it to give access to the lower hide, which is considerably higher at 1.9m.

The gateway towers at Coughton Court

This scheme sounds effective, but it can be seen from the photo-graph above that the right-hand tower has a long stretch of windowless wall which is not duplicated on the left. This would have given the pursuivants a clue. As the *Narrative* warned: 'They do also measure the walls of the house and go round about the house on the outside to see if one part do answer to another.'[16] It was no doubt the inadequacy of this scheme which impelled Nicholas and Garnet to move to Hindlip.

It has been suggested that the hide was formed from a garderobe downshaft, but firstly the dimensions seem ridiculously large for such a purpose and secondly, as Squiers has pointed out, it is on the opposite side of the tower from the moat, so any drainage tunnel would have to go under the whole building. A possibility is that it once contained a narrow spiral staircase for the use of the servants.

Huddington Court

One more hide-within-a-hide can be mentioned, because it exemplifies yet another method of constructing priest-holes and also because of the importance of its location. This is Huddington Court, once the home of the Wintour brothers who were prime movers in the Gunpowder Plot. Huddington lies roughly between Coughton Court and Hindlip House and as it was a major recusant house in the area, Nicholas is almost certainly the man that constructed its priest-holes. There is more than one hide at Huddington, but the one we are concerned with lies within the complex of garret rooms in one wing. It can be seen from the illustration above that there are two conjoined blocks, one lying a little lower than the other.

The clandestine chapel lay in the garret room of one block. The hide is situated in the upper part of the garret of the second block, and the inner hide within a dormer on the second block. The main entrance is a camouflaged panel within the wainscoting, giving access to a spacious priest-hole. This was the main place of concealment, but if the pursuivants seemed to be about to break in, there was yet another camouflaged panel giving access to the inner hide, where the hunted priest could crouch with his knees to his chest.

Again, the weakness of this system is that all the gables can be seen from the outside and a careful check would show that there were missing areas.

It would be tedious to enumerate every variation that priest-hole designers used; suffice it to say that they were many and usually ingenious. We will however look at just one more, because it is now unique of its type. The *True Discovery* manuscript relating the story of the search at Hindlip House, describes priest-holes built into chimneys, in one of which Garnet and Oldcorne were found. It runs:

> These chimney-conveyances being so strangely formed, having the entrances into them so curiously covered over with brick, mortared and made fast to planks of wood, and coloured black, like the other parts of the chimney, that very diligent inquisition might well have passed by, without throwing the least suspicion upon such unsuspicious places. And whereas divers funnels are usually made to chimneys according as they are combined together, and serve for necessary use in several rooms, so here were some that exceeded common expectation, seeming outwardly fit for carrying forth smoke; but being further examined and seen into, their service was to no such purpose but only to lend air and light downward into the concealments, where such as were concealed in them, at any time should be hidden.

There is now only one surviving example of this, which is at Irnham Hall in Lincolnshire. The picture opposite shows the cylindrical ventilating chimney in the middle of the photograph. A genuine chimney is on the left.

The windowed gable in the foreground contains the small chapel. There are three steps leading down into the chapel and one of these can be raised so that in the event of a raid the massing stuff and vestments could be thrown down into the hide and the priest himself then climb down.

The hide itself is on the floor below, behind the wall of a large bedroom. It is quite spacious at 2.5m by 1.2m and 1.6m high. On one side is a hole leading to a small chamber directly below the chimney. It is likely that this served as the latrine for the priest-hole.

The old chapel at Irnham Hall

When it was discovered in 1844, it was said to have a feeding tube into the adjacent bedroom, as was used in Garnet's hide at Hindlip. Given this 'hallmark' together with the hinged stair entrance as used at Harvington Hall, we can be confident this is one of Nicholas' designs.

It has been generally assumed that Nicholas also built the chimney itself. However, I feel that given that it is very conspicuous, being of considerable size and also being cylindrical where all the other chimneys are rectangular, that it is more likely that it was an existing feature which Nicholas adapted to his own purposes.

There is a popular idea, that can be traced back to Granville Squiers' book, that Nicholas almost always provided a second exit from his hides for emergency use when the pursuivants were about to break in. In fact, this arrangement is very much a rarity. It is clear that having two access points would double the chances of discovery and given that up to a hundred men were deployed in searches, making a dash for it from an exit only a few metres away would almost certainly be futile. Squiers claims to have seen evidence of a second exit at Braddocks and Oxburgh Hall, but there is certainly nothing of the sort to be seen now. Hodgetts has recorded that at Harvington Hall visitors have speculated that the extra thickness of the wall at the back of the stair hide indicates that there was once an emergency exit at this point; he is however of the opinion that this was necessitated by the need to make good following demolition of an adjacent building.[17]

Two priest-holes that it seems may indeed have had a second entrance (although today there is no clear evidence) are at Coughton Court, where the double hide down the tower may have once had access at the bottom as well as the top, and the other is another priest-hole at Huddington Court where Nicholas erected a false wall that divided off a sizeable section of a garret room. Here, there is an indication that entrances were provided from the rooms on either side of the priest-hole. It is noteworthy that in both these cases the entrances are in quite different parts of the building: at Coughton on a separate floor and at Huddington in a room with a separate staircase accessing it.

We can occasionally assign a date to Nicholas' work. The hide at Braddocks, for example, we can say with confidence was excavated at Christmas 1592, because the deposition of the traitor John Frank states that Nicholas was present at that time. Also, at Baddesley Clinton we are confident that Nicholas worked to build the sewer hide in the winter of 1589–90. Both of these are 'early Nicholas.' The hides near the Great Staircase at Harvington Hall were almost certainly built when the staircase was installed after 1600, in the last five years of Nicholas' life. We see him here at the height of his powers.

In other cases, we have to fall back on deduction. It is, for instance, generally supposed that the hide at Sawston Hall was constructed soon after the one at Braddocks, only 18 km. away. The reason for this is that Mrs Wiseman's brother, who lived at Sawston, was reconciled to Catholicism by Gerard at that time and a hide would have been built for the use of a resident priest. However, it is clear that the Sawston hide is far more sophisticated than the one at Braddocks. For sanitation, Braddocks has a crude concave section chiselled into the brickwork to give enough room for a close-stool, where Sawston has a proper latrine. It has ventilation where Braddocks has none; although it would have been possible to arrange something through a nearby flue. Most importantly, Braddocks had a very flimsy arrangement for concealment consisting of bricks laid loose on timber, which burnt away and very nearly betrayed Gerard. Nicholas was capable of much better than this. As we have seen, at Oxburgh Hall he created a very sturdy cap to the priest-hole which had tiles fitted securely to it with an iron frame. A solution such as this would have stood up to the fire. I would hypothesise that Nicholas did indeed build a priest-hole at Sawston around 1593, but it was not the stair hide described above. There are other hides at Sawston and it is likely that Nicholas paid more than one visit and constructed the stair hide at a later date when he had improved his skills.

It is pleasing to consider that we may well see more priest-holes rediscovered. In an episode evoking innumerable scenes from children's fiction, the ingenious pivoting beam hide at Harvington was discovered by a young boy in 1897 when he teased out a loose brick. Similarly, the double hide at Coughton Court, despite its considerable size, was forgotten and found only during repair work in 1945. We can have every hope that more examples of Nicholas' particular genius remain to be found.

THE RACK

Torture and Death

On the first occasion that Nicholas was captured, twelve years previously, the authorities had not realised that they had anyone of importance in their clutches. This time it was different. No doubt through confessions wrung out on the rack they knew that Nicholas was the chief builder of priest-holes in England. One Councillor (Tesimond says it was the Earl of Salisbury himself) exulted: 'Is he taken that knows all the secret places? I am very glad of that. We will have a trick for him.'[1]

When he was first brought to London, he was taken to the Marshalsea prison where he was kept under light confinement and allowed visitors. This, his friends believed, was a ruse to see who came to visit him and overhear what was said. Nicholas, however, was too cautious to be tricked: as Tesimond says, 'when Owen realised this he broke off relations with everyone he knew'[2] and spent his time preparing for the ordeal he would have to undergo.

Astonishingly, Garnet and Oldcorne were compromised by a similar trick in their prison at the Gatehouse. They were in separate cells and their keeper, who seems to have been chosen for his acting ability, purported to be sympathetic to their plight and personally impressed by the virtues of Father Garnet. He offered to take letters to and fro but when this was accepted delivered them first to the Lieutenant of the Tower who, as described earlier, read them, had copies made and passed them on. The gaoler also, saying that he would like to do the priests a favour provided they promised not to tell anyone, showed them a crack in the wall by which they might speak to one another. But:

> the place was purposely so contrived as that the sound of their words must needs be carried to another place not far off, where this keeper* would stand and some other with him, to have a double witness in their double dealing.[3]

By this means the authorities gathered a good deal of information, some of which was used against them at their trials.

After some time, both Nicholas and Henry Garnet were trans-ferred to the Tower of London. Garnet was treated relatively well, and his friends were allowed to supply him with wine and other small comforts. Nicholas, however, they marked for torture. Topcliffe had died two years earlier, but the Tower had no shortage of merciless rackmasters.

Many rotted in that place for years. This inscription can still be seen in the Beauchamp Tower: *Quanto plus afflictionis pro Christo in hoc saeculo, tanto plus gloriae cum Christo in futuro. Arundell - 22 June 1587* – 'The more affliction we endure for Christ in this world, the more glory we shall get with Christ in the world to come'. It was carved by the Earl of Arundel who spent the rest of his life in the Beauchamp Tower. As he lay dying, he petitioned the Queen that he might see his wife and son one last time. Elizabeth replied: 'If he but once would go to [the Protestant] Church, his request should not only be granted, but he should be restored to his honour and estates with as much favour as she could show.' To this, the Earl responded that 'He could not accept Her Majesty's offer upon that condition [and] he was sorry he had but one life to lose in such a cause.'[5]

There is some doubt as to the legality of torture. Queen Elizabeth's Secretary of State, Sir Thomas Smith, boasted that 'torment or question which is used by the order of the civill lawe and custome of other countreis to put a malefactor to excessive paine ... is not used in England.'[6]

---

* The *Narrative* seems to be mistaken in detail about this. The gaoler's name was Carey, but the names signed on the report are Edward Forsett and John Locherson.[4]

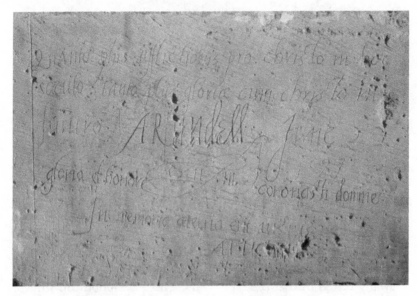

The inscription in the Beauchamp Tower
(courtesy Historic Royal Palaces)

This is a disingenuous statement, turning on the mention of 'the civil law.' It is true that ordinary courts had no power to authorise torture, but the monarch retained the power to do so through Royal Warrant, as did the Privy Council through its judicial arm, the Court of Star Chamber.

The majority of recorded cases that we have are Elizabethan, and Sir Thomas is known to have been involved in at least some of them. It appears that the most common form of torture at this time was not the rack but the manacles, or strappado, where the victim is suspended by his wrists, perhaps with a weight tied to his legs. As we have seen, Nicholas and Richard Fulwood were tortured at the Poultry on the earlier arrest, being 'hung up for three hours together, having their arms fixed into iron rings, and their bodies hanging in the air.' For the more important prisoners a formal procedure was followed. When John Gerard was committed to the Tower after it was found that he was sending and receiving letters by Nicholas, a warrant was sent to the Lieutenant of the Tower, the latter part of which ran:

if you shall finde him obstinate, undutyfull or unwilling to declare and reveale the thruthe as he ought to do by his duty and allegeaunce, you shall by vertue hereof cause him to be put to the manacles and suche other torture as is used in that place, that he maie be forced to utter directlie and truly his uttermost knowledg in all these thinges that maie any waie concerne her Majesty and the State and are meet to be knowne.[7]

In the current circumstances the Privy Council decided to dispense with the red tape. On the 22nd February, about the time when Nicholas would have been committed, it wrote to the Lieutenant who was then Sir William Wade, regarding prisoners detained in connection with the 'Powder Treason' giving him general power to 'put the inferior prisoners to the rack.'[8] Wade would undoubtedly have placed Nicholas in this category.

The *Narrative* states that as Nicholas had a hernia, it was against the law to torture him, saying: 'the man had a rupture in his belly ... and a man in that case is so unable to abide torments, that the civil law doth forbid to torture any man that is broken.'[9] Again, this is not correct as the civil law had no authority to impose torture in any circumstances. It is likely however that it was customary not to torture people with severe disabilities for the practical reason that they were more likely to die and so cause embarrassment. The authorities knew that Nicholas was potentially one of the best sources of information they had ever had, and were determined to make him speak.

Quite early on Nicholas gave a 'confession' in which he denied knowing anything or anyone, with the exception of Ralph Ashley who had been captured with him, and even then he stuck to Ralph's alias of 'George Chambers.' A report sent to the Council dated February 26, 1606 says:

He confesseth that he hath been called by the name of Andrewes and knoweth not whether he hath bene called by the name of Little John, or Draper, or any other name than Owen and Andrewes.

That he came to Mr Abington's house the Saturday before he was taken, but refuseth to answer from which place he came.

He denieth that he knoweth Father Garnett or that he ever served him, or that he (Father Garnett) is called by the name of Mease, Darcy, Whalley, Philips, Fermor, or any other name.

He denieth that he knoweth a Jesuit called Oldcorne, or Hall.
And that he knoweth that Geo. Chambers served Hall the Jesuite.
He confesseth that he hath known George Chambers some six or
seven years, and become acquainted with him at an ordinarie [eating
house] in Fleet Street and saith he, this examinant served at that
tyme Mr Henry Drurie of Sussex.[10]

The interrogators would hardly be satisfied with this and continued
the torture as far as we can tell every day for the next three days.
Nicholas was hung in the manacles daily and for hours at a time.
The author of the *Narrative* must have been close enough to receive
daily reports or may even have been a prisoner himself, as he
records that:

he hung in the torture seven hours together, and this divers times,
though we cannot as yet learn the certain number, but day after day
we heard of his being carried to torments.[11]

Father Tesimond's Italian version of the *Narrative* expands on this
somewhat, saying:

They tormented him with hideous cruelty. Every day, news arrived
of freshly devised tortures which he had to suffer, and this went on
for many days continually; but the truth is, we do not know the
details even to this day. All we know is that, sometimes for several
hours on end, he was subjected to torture. The only sound to be
heard from him was one which had long been familiar with him at all
hours and times, 'Sweet Jesus!' and 'Lord, give me your holy grace
and patience!'[12]

The rackmaster had a practical problem because the torture caused
Nicholas' hernia to gape and his intestines to bulge out through his
abdominal wall. Sustaining a rupture on the manacles or rack was
a common occurrence. Father Tesimond notes that 'in the course of
torture of that kind, the stomach is apt to swell, and suffers more
severe pain and distension than other parts of the body'[13] and Father
Thomas Pormont, who was racked in 1592 by Topcliffe and
famously revealed the pursuivant's intimacies with the Queen,
suffered this injury. The solution hit upon was to tie a circular

metal plate over the hernia as a sort of primitive truss. The *Narrative* describes it thus:

> He, therefore, being not only tortured, but that with so much extremity and so long continuance, it could not be otherwise but that his bowels should come out; which, when they perceived, and minding as yet to continue that course with him, they girded his belly with a plate of iron to keep in his bowels.[14]

The image below is taken from Tanner's *Martyres* and shows Nicholas in the manacles with a weight tied to his ankles. It's not likely to be historically accurate, not least because it shows Nicholas as of normal height.

Nicolaus Odöenus Anglus Soc:IESU. odio Religionis Catholicæ tormentis enectus Londini in Anglia A. 1606 12 Nouembris.

The examination of Nicholas Owen from Tanner's Martyres

After three days of this, on March 1ˢᵗ, Nicholas was prepared to say that he had occasionally served Garnet over the last four years. He told them nothing useful: Throckmorton had rented out Coughton Court and had then circumspectly gone abroad; he could therefore plausibly deny knowledge of what went on there; Lady Mary Digby's husband Everard had been executed for treason two months previously; Catesby and Percy had been killed by musket-shot in the days after the Plot was discovered, and White Webbs was considered 'blown' the year before.

The record of the confession runs:

He confesseth that he hath at tymes attended and followed Henry Garnett, the Provincial of the Jesuits, some fower yeares or there-abouts.

That he was at the house of Thomas Throgmorton called Coughton, in the beginning of November last, when the Ladie Digby was there, and by the watch that was in the town they did under-stand that Catesby, Percy, and the rest of the traytors were upp in armes.

That on All Hallowe Day last, Garnett did say Masse at Coughton House, at which Masse this examinant was, and some others to the number of half a dozen.

That the forenamed Henry Garnett als. Walley, the Provincial, was at Henlipp, the house of Thos. Abington, some six weeks before the tyme that he was apprehended by Sir Henry Bromley; and Hall [Oldcorne] the Jesuite was there about three days before the house of Mr Abington was besett, having been there also before that tyme, and from thence the said Hall went into the country for the space of a seven night, and same againe as before is said, some three days before the house was besett.

That during the foresaid time of 6 weeks he did attend on Mr Garnett to make his fyer and to do those things which were fitt about him. That the said Garnett did lye in a lower chamber descend-ing from the dyning roome; and did ordinarily dyne and sup in the dyning chamber with Mr Abington and his wife; and when Hall was there, he did dyne and sup there likewise.

He also doth confesse that he hath bene often tymes with the said Garnett at the house called White Webbs, in Enfield Chase.

Taken by W. Waad [Sir William Wade], John Corbett, etc.[15]

They got nothing more from him. Later that same day he was put to the torture again and died in the most agonising manner. As far as it is possible to tell, the stretching of his body forced his hernia out past the metal plate and the edge of it gashed the intestines so severely that he perished. The description in the *Narrative* says that the torture 'did force out his guts, and so the iron did serve but to cut and wound his body'.[16]

It is possible that as the manacles had not persuaded him to talk, the authorities decided to put him on the rack and the greater power of that device, using a windlass rather than the force of gravity, burst his abdomen. The Tower had followed this sequence some months earlier when interrogating Guy Fawkes. When put to the 'gentler tortures' Fawkes had said very little but after four days Wade was able to write to Cecil blandly announcing that he had a full confession after 'plying him with the best persuasions I could use.'[17]

Even by the standards of the time, a death in this manner was embarrassing.* The authorities decided to give out that Nicholas had committed suicide with a knife given to him by his warder so that he could cut his food. The *Narrative* speculates that the fact that his belly had been slashed by the metal plate gave them that idea. A formal inquest was held and a verdict of *felo-de-se* (suicide) was returned. One of the King's Chaplains, Dr. Robert Abbott, wrote the official account of his death, including unlikely circumstantial detail in which his keeper treated him with every kindness and Nicholas confessed with his dying breath that he had stabbed himself.

The next day, he complained of illness to his keeper, who humanely carried him a chair to use at his dinner, and with his food a blunt-pointed knife was as usual brought for the purpose of cutting his meat. Owen pretended to find fault with the coldness of his broth, and besought the keeper to put it on the fire for him in an adjoining

---

* In a booklet on Nicholas,[18] Father Caraman gives an extract from a letter of instruction from Salisbury to the Attorney General, Sir Edward Coke, on March 28th which runs: 'You must remember to lay Owen as foul in this as you can.'[19] Most authorities however believe that this reference is to Hugh Owen, a soldier of fortune in Flanders, who had been in contact with Guy Fawkes.

apartment; and as soon as the man had left the cell for this purpose, he seized the opportunity of ripping up his belly in a frightful manner with the knife. The keeper on his return, observing the pale and ghastly countenance of the prisoner, and perceiving blood sprinkled on the floor threw off the straw which the unfortunate man had drawn over him, and discovered what had happened. He then ran to inform the lieutenant, who immediately hastened to the cell with several guests who happened to be at dinner with him. In answer to their questions, the dying man declared that he had committed the act of self-destruction entirely from the apprehension of severer torture than he had suffered the day before.[20]

To bolster the story further, the authorities had an illustrated ballad published showing Nicholas 'ripping out his own bowels with a knife as he lay in bed, his keeper being also in the chamber busy about some other thing.'[21] Ballads were a common propaganda tool at the time. They were sold very cheaply and usually featured a woodcut and new words set to a well-known tune so that the common people could edify and entertain themselves with song.

The illustration overleaf shows such a ballad reviling the Gunpowder Plot to the tune of *Aim Not Too High*. The thrust (and general quality) of the ballad is well given by the verse:

> To their old plotting Trade they strait did go,
> To prove Three Kingdom's final Overthrow,
> A Plot contriv'd by Catholicks alone;
> The like before or since was never known.

The Jesuit historian Daniello Bartoli says that Nicholas' body was put on display so that the wounds on his stomach could be witnessed. He writes that 'they exposed his body to be seen by people, who arrived in numbers to damn his soul or to mock him.'[22] Bartoli was writing sixty years later, but gives as his authority a letter written on the 13th March, only eleven days after the death. This letter was from Father William Baldwin then living in Brussels. Baldwin was regularly visited by priests from England and would pass on news to Robert Persons, rector of the English College in Rome. This letter now appears to have been lost, but on the whole the action described seems unlikely: it was not the custom to display bodies in such a manner at the Tower, and the pitiable sight

GUN-POWDER Plot:

OR,

A Brief Account of that bloudy and subtle Defign laid againft the King, his Lords and Commons in Parliament, and of a Happy Deliverance by Divine Power.

To the Tune of *Aim not too high.*   Licenfed according to Order.

Westminster.

A broadside ballad

(courtesy Magdalene College)

of Nicholas' diminutive and mutilated corpse would be more likely to evoke sympathy than mockery.

We can deduce the date of Nicholas' death from other sources. Sir Edward Hoby, a Member of Parliament, wrote a letter to a diplomat in which he says:

> The second of March one Oven [margin: he was nicknamed Anderos and little Dike, servant to Garnet] ... killed him selfe in the Tower, ripping up his owne belly with a knife without a pointe.[23]

We also have a record of Star Chamber proceedings a few months later against two Catholics who were uttering 'treasonable speech concerning the death of Owen.' The indictment runs:

That whereas Henry Owen [sic] servant to Henry Garnett clerk lately
of high treason attainted was in or near about the beginning of
February last past by order and direction of the Lords of Your
Highness' Privy Council committed to the Tower of London upon
suspicion of the late most horrible treasons of blowing up the Parliament House with powder ... That on the first day of March last past
one James Fitzjames of Redlynch in the county of Somerset, gent.,
being a recusant and ill-affected in religion, did meet with one
Edward Prater of Nunney Castle in the county of Somerset, gent., a
recusant also and ill-affected in religion, and then and there
demanded of the said Edward Prater, What news? Whereunto Prater
answered he knew none. Thereupon James Fitzjames falsely ... did
... inform the said Prater that he had been that day at the Tower at
Sir John Timothy, and then most falsely said and declared unto the
said Prater that he had heard there from the same Sir John Timothy
that a servant to one of the priests or to Mr Abington [of Hindlip] he
knew not whether, (without declaring his name) was tortured to
death. And where also the said Henry Owen knowing himself to be
guilty of the said most horrible treasons and fearing the execution of
Justice against him for the same, being thereunto most wickedly
seduced by the instigation of the devil, did upon the second day of
March last past most desperately and devilishly murder and kill
himself in the said prison of the Tower of London.

    ... That the said Edward Prater, being on the fourth day of March
last past at dinner in the company of divers gents. and others at the
lodgings of Sir Hugh Pollard, knight, in your Majesty's house called
St John's near unto Clerkenwell ... and hearing the said Sir Hugh
Pollard then say that a prisoner in the Tower (meaning the said
Henry Owen) had killed himself, he the said Edward Prater... did
then and there most falsely answer that he heard that the said
prisoner... was tortured to death. Whereupon, reply being made by
the Lady Pollard that he killed himself, for, as she said, it was
generally reported so everywhere, he the said Edward Prater did
then and there offer to lay a wager with her that the same prisoner
was tortured to death.[24]

We also have a despatch from the Venetian ambassador, Zorzi Giustinian, to his government. It deals with various matters and was
written partly in cipher, which is given here in italics. The passage
that concerns us runs:

I ought to add that while the King [James] was talking to me he let fall that last night one of the Jesuits, conscience-stricken for his sins, stabbed himself deeply in the body twice with a knife. When the warders ran up at the noise they found him still alive. He confessed to having taken a share in the Plot at the suggestion of his Provincial, and now, recognising his crime, he had resolved to kill himself, and so escape the terrible death that overhung him, as he deserved. *Public opinion, however, holds that he died of the tortures inflicted on him, which were so severe that they deprived him not only of his strength, but of the power to move any part of his body, and so they think it unlikely that he should have been able to stab himself in the body, especially with a blunt knife, as they allege. It is thought that as he confessed nothing and is dead, they have hoodwinked the King himself by publishing this account* in order to rouse him and everybody to greater animosity against the Catholics and to make the case blacker against his companion the Provincial.[25]

The despatch is dated March 23rd 1606, three weeks after Nicholas' death: it is likely that Giustinian updated his reports daily and sent them at convenient times.

We therefore have a slight discrepancy in dates between the 1st and 2nd of March 1606, but from Giustinian's words of 'last night' (*la notte precedente*) it would seem that Nicholas died in the night between those dates, but the news was not generally known until the next morning. Abdominal injuries are often not immediately fatal and it is possible that Nicholas lingered on in agony for some hours before he finally expired. On the other hand, Bartoli, presumably getting his information from Baldwin's letter, says that 'the bowels that had been squeezed by this torment came out on one side; and [Nicholas] immediately died of the unbearable pain.'[26]

Giustinian's guess that the King himself was not told the truth may well be accurate. Bartoli also claims that the matter was covered up:

in order to bury and hide such an event, that was not only atrocious but also reeked of barbarity, that would have displeased the King as it was offensive and contrary to the principles of clemency he professed.[27]

The author of the *Narrative* spends four pages denying that Nicholas committed suicide. The reason for such vehemence is clear: according to Catholic doctrine, suicide is a 'mortal' sin and by dying unabsolved Nicholas would be condemned to hell. He firstly points out that knives supplied to prisoners are never able to stab, for obvious reasons, and can only cut. He also says that a kinswoman of Nicholas asked the warder to get from his prisoner a written list of what he needed. The reply was: 'What would you have him write? He is not able to put on his own cap: no, not to feed himself, but I am forced to feed him.'[28] Nicholas therefore would not have been able to wield a knife in any event.

We can make a guess as to the identity of the 'kinswoman.' It appears that Henry Owen had married, for we have a record that on the 7th February 1601, *Ellinora Oven uxor Henrici Oven* (Ellen Owen, wife of Henry Owen) of Wendlebury, 12 km. from Oxford, was excommunicated from the established Church for recusancy.[29] Since his spell in the Clink with Gerard, Henry had continued with his work of printing books and other articles in support of the faith and was imprisoned for it at various times. In the previous year, 1605, he had been arrested again in London.[30] It therefore seems likely that it was Nicholas' sister-in-law Ellen who was visiting him and bringing him comforts. Henry himself was probably still in prison at that date.

Ellen also received the news of his death from the gaoler. The *Narrative* records that:

> But afterwards, the same party, seeking further to know his estate, and coming to the keeper to learn, as desirous to help him with anything that was needful, he secretly wished her to trouble herself no more, for, said he, 'The man is dead, he died in our hands.' [31]

The account puts forward the argument that if he had decided to yield to sin, he would rather than kill himself have sold the informa-tion he had. It is pointed out that he could:

> have made it almost an impossible thing for Priests to escape, knowing the residences of most Priests in England, and of all those of the Society, whom he might have taken as partridges in a net, knowing all their secret places which himself had made, and the like

conveyances in most of the chief Catholics' houses in England, and the means and manner how all such places were to be found, though made by others.[32]

It then goes on to describe the amount of money to be made, because on arresting the priests in recusant homes, the government would also be entitled to seize the entire estate of the families that sheltered them. Nicholas would have got his cut and become a rich man. As the manuscript says:

> He might have made himself great in the world, not only by their rewards for so great and extraordinary service, but also by the spoil of Catholics' goods, being so many and so great, as he might have come to the rifling of, and have had no doubt much thereof for his own share.[33]

All this seems rather strange: Nicholas was of proven loyalty and would never have betrayed the priests he served and his fellow-Catholics for any amount of money.

The account concludes with what would be the most important issue for Nicholas as for any orthodox Catholic:

> If he would have swallowed the hook of sin for the avoiding of torment, than by the torment of death voluntarily assumed, not to end his torments, as he well knew, but to begin a never-ending and that also much more intolerable torment in hell-fire.[34]

The last word can be John Gerard's. His summary is in the version of the *Narrative* in his handwriting but not in Father Tesimond's account, so we can be sure they are his own beliefs:

> The truth was this: the man had lived a saintly life, and his death was answerable, and he a glorious martyr of extraordinary merit. God assisted him with so much grace that in all his torments he gave not the least sign of relenting, not any sign of impatience, not any one word by which the least of his acquaintance either did or might come in any trouble.[35]

PAUL VI

The Forty Martyrs

According to Henry More, the great-grandson of Thomas More and an early historian of the Jesuits, Nicholas was buried *in ipsa arce*: 'in the citadel.'[1] This must mean the church of St Peter ad Vincula within the walls of the Tower. (This, incidentally, is further evidence that his death was not by suicide, as suicides were normally buried on unconsecrated ground with a stake driven through them to pin them to the earth and stop them 'walking.')

The church had a small graveyard on the south side, which is now laid to lawn. If there should be an archaeological dig at the site, his short stature and broken leg might identify him, but it is much more likely in ground lying so close to the Thames that his mortal remains have now disappeared.

Henry Garnet, Nicholas' master for eighteen years, was put on trial for High Treason. His defence that the seal of the confessional prevented him from revealing that there was a plot against the King's life was met with 'great laughter' in court. The jury took less than fifteen minutes to find him guilty and he was sentenced to be hung, drawn and quartered. Two months after Nicholas had died, Henry Garnet was drawn on a hurdle to St Paul's churchyard. This spot was not usually used for executions and some thought the arrangement sacrilegious, but Salisbury wanted to imply a parallel between the place of rejoicing at the defeat of the Armada and the death of one whom the government claimed had plotted against the life of the present monarch.

St Peter ad Vincula
(courtesy Historic Royal Palaces)

His execution drew an immense crowd, with spectators having to pay twelvepence just to stand on a wall.[2] The ordinary person had been taught to fear Jesuits as evil, devious and traitorous and their Superior as a veritable Prince of Darkness. There was much speech at the foot of the scaffold with various officials trying to get him to confess to treason and others trying to convert him. Eventually he was required to ascend a ladder which the hangman then pulled away. When he had suffered strangulation for a short time the hangman made as if to cut him down for castration and disembowelment, but the crowd was, or had become, sympathetic to him and 'prevented the hangman with a loud cry that he might not cut him down too soon.' The hangman tried again a short while later but 'the people cried out again, "Hold, hold," and so again the third time, not permitting him to be cut down until he was thoroughly dead.'[3]

P.Henricus Garnettus Anglus Soc: IESU. Religionis Catholicæ
odio suspensus et sectus Londini in Anglia. A. 1606. 3 May

The execution of Henry Garnet, from Tanner's Martyres

After his execution, Garnet's skin was flayed and used to bind
one of the copies of a book detailing the speeches and evidence at his
trial. It was entitled: *A True and Perfect Relation of the Whole
Proceedings Against the Late Most Barbarous Traitors, Garnet A
Jesuit and His Confederates.* This volume still exists and was
auctioned in recent years.[4]

Of the others captured with Nicholas and Garnet, Edward
Oldcorne and his servant Ralph Ashley were sent back to Worcester
to be tried at the assizes and were subsequently executed at the
nearby village of Redhill. Thomas Habington, the owner of Hindlip
House, was convicted of harbouring priests but his life was spared
on condition he never again left Worcestershire. He prudently
devoted the rest of his life to antiquarian research.

John Gerard found England too hot to hold him after the Plot was discovered. He was known to have associated with the conspirators and Robert Cecil himself was taking a personal interest in his capture.[5] His houses and those of his friends were raided again and again. Finally, he decided to escape to the Continent which he did on May 3rd 1606, disguised as a member of the Spanish Ambassador's entourage. His superiors set him to train Jesuit novices who were to carry on his work in England and on their orders he wrote his *Autobiography* and also prepared the English translation of the *Narrative of the Gunpowder Plot*, both of which have given us so much information.

Nicholas' father, Walter, died the next year in 1607. His brother John was arrested in 1618 and convicted of treason. His life was spared on condition that he went into exile abroad. Nothing more is known of him.

His other surviving brother, Henry, is known to have continued his work of printing Catholic books. He is recorded as being active in Bethnal Green, in east London in 1616,[6] when he would have been about forty-five years old.

It is generally assumed that Nicholas at some point in his service was formally made a co-adjutor, or lay-brother of the Jesuits. This is however far from certain.

Tanner's *Martyres*, written long after Nicholas' death, says that he was made a lay-brother, but it was kept quiet because other more high-born Catholics would be envious. Tanner writes:

Father Garnett ... received his solemn profession in the Society; but the Fathers studiously concealed the fact of his being a lay-brother, lest a door of entrance to that degree should seem to have been opened for men of the highest rank ... for the religious virtues of Brother Owen, notwithstanding all his efforts to play the servant, shone so clearly forth from beneath the disguise, that great men became envious of his state, and eagerly solicited admission to it from Father Garnett, the Superior.[7]

We have seen before, however, that modern scholarship has shown that Tanner is mistaken in some important facts.

Henry Foley's *Records of the English Province of the Society of*

Jesus, written in Victorian times, takes Tanner as his source but adds some research of his own to bolster the matter, saying:

> Father Tanner's 'lawful binding to the Society' would, no doubt, refer to Owen's solemn profession, which is never allowed until after at least a trial of ten or twelve years. ... In 1580, Father General wrote several letters of consolation to some of the suffering English members, and amongst others one addressed 'To our Brother Nicholas.' He was clearly admitted at that time.[8]

This deduction cannot be correct as in 1580 Nicholas Owen was in the first years of his apprenticeship. Recent research has found that a Jesuit called Nicholas Smith was in England at that time[9] – it is probably he to whom that letter is addressed.

Turning to contemporary sources, the author of the *Narrative* thinks that he was admitted but is not completely certain, writing a few years after Nicholas' death:

> as we generally think a Lay-coadjutor of the Society, admitted by Father Garnett some years before his death, though his humble and discreet carriage was such as you could not discern any liberty of fellowlike conversation that he took thereupon with any of the Society, but rather carried himself in all things as a servant. And I have some reasons more in particulars to think that he was assuredly admitted of the Order, yet those can better tell that are of the Society here in England.[10]

The first we hear of the subject is in a letter from Garnet to Aquaviva in 1599 in which he says:

> I am employing certain people who wish to be coadjutors. All are of the highest reputation and they help me as much as if they had already been admitted among us... They serve us excellently in the hope that before they die they will be at least Coadjutors. ... I keep one joiner for making secret places in which to hide our money and other things of importance.[11]

It is clear therefore both that Nicholas was not at that time a co-adjutor and that Father Garnet, despite being the senior Jesuit in England, did not consider that he had the power to admit lay-

brothers on his own authority. It might seem strange to those unac-
quainted with the iron discipline which the Jesuits impose upon
themselves that there should be any doubt about Nicholas'
admission. He had at the time of this letter served his priest faith-
fully for eleven years, built refuges that had saved many lives and
suffered imprisonment and torture without betraying any harmful
information.

The last letter Garnet ever wrote to his superiors in Rome was
addressed to Robert Persons, who had been appointed by Aquaviva
to take responsibility for English affairs. In this, he asks again for
permission to take his servants into the Society. 'Pray you send
word now how many coadjutors you will have,' he writes. He pleads
especially for John Lillie, saying: 'I have one, a citizen of London, of
very good experience.'[12] Nicholas is not mentioned, but Lillie was
five years older and as an administrator would be considered the
more senior man. It was he that led the team that rescued Gerard
from the Tower. In addition, the length of his service was at least
comparable with Nicholas' – we first hear of him from Garnet in
1590. It is surely unlikely that Nicholas was a co-adjutor if Lillie
was not.

There would barely have been time for Persons to receive this
letter (dated the 4th October 1605 but despatched at the end of the
month), still less for a reply to have been received by Garnet before
his capture. Sadly then, it seems on the evidence that Nicholas Owen
was never a lay-brother. We can perhaps take consolation from the
thought that being declared a saint and martyr is an even higher
honour than being accepted as a member of the Society of Jesus.

In all, the persecution lasted for over a century: from 1535 when
Thomas More was executed on the orders of Henry VIII, to 1679
when Titus Oates whipped up an entirely fictitious story that the
Jesuits were organising the assassination of Charles II and popular
outrage resulted in further deaths.

In legal terms, the persecution ended when James II ascended the
throne in 1685. James was the brother of Charles II but his ascension
was unpopular as he had converted to Catholicism. However, his
right to the throne, given that Charles had died without legitimate
offspring, was clear. Under James, Parliament passed the *Declaration of Indulgence* Act which, amongst other matters, ended the

fines for not attending Anglican worship. Despite this, a range of Penal Laws placed restrictions on Catholics until well into the nine-teenth century, with them for example not being allowed to attend university, practice law or medicine, be officers in the Army or Navy or hold any public office, including being a Member of Parlia-ment. The echoes of the Bloody Question resonated down the centuries: in the end, was the loyalty of Catholics to the Crown or to Rome?

The Catholic Church favours giving recognition to those who in life served the faith in some exceptional way, so that their example may be an inspiration to others. There are up to three steps in the process: a candidate being in turn declared 'Venerable', 'Blessed' and finally a Saint. It is usual that nominations for this recognition, accompanied by bound volumes of evidence of sanctity, come from a local level, but this was not possible at the time because the old diocesan structure had collapsed in the time of Elizabeth with the death of the last Marian bishop in 1585.

In 1643 Urban VIII, at the request of the English Benedictines in exile, appointed a commission of English priests to prepare a submission under the direction of the Archbishop of Cambrai in northern France. However, the English authorities got to know of this and frustrated all attempts to collect evidence.

So matters rested for over two hundred years. In the late eigh-teenth century there were probably only about 80,000 Catholics in England, generally in the north of the country:[13] a little over 1% of the population. In most cases the faith survived in small pockets, where a local land-owning recusant family was able to protect its villagers and servants. For the greater part of this period governance of the Catholic community was through four 'apostolic vicars', each responsible for a very large area.

With the gradual easing of restrictions, numbers were able to grow through conversion and with immigration, especially of Irish Catholics, so that in 1850 Pope Pius IX was able to issue the bull *Universalis Ecclesiae* ('The Universal Church') recreating the diocesan hierarchy and appointing bishops to their Sees.

It was now practicable to prepare a submission to the Vatican to give formal honour and recognition to those who had died for their faith during the Persecution. The administrative process changed in

1969, but at the time of which we're speaking the procedure was superintended by the papal Congregation of Rites. Once a petition, or Cause, was accepted, the Congregation would appoint a Postulator to put forward the case for the candidate and also a person to challenge the nomination. The latter is formally entitled the Defender of the Faith, but is famously dubbed the 'Devil's Advocate'.

Initial preparations began a few years after the reinstatement of the hierarchy, but due to the large numbers of those put forward it was not until 1886 that the Cause of 254 of those seen as being the most deserving was introduced. Some fell by the wayside for lack of evidence or because death could have been by natural causes, even while imprisoned, but finally the Congregation of Rites felt that there was enough evidence to grant the 'admission of the Cause' of 241 martyrs, including Nicholas, who could now be titled 'Venerable'.

Detailed examinations of each candidate followed. Finally, a full forty-three years after the introduction of the Cause, the Congregation was able to send a recommendation to the Pope that 136 of the candidates put forward were worthy of beatification[14] and on the 15th December 1929, Pius XI with the Apostolic Letter *Atrocissima tormenta passi* ('cruel punishment') made the formal declaration. Nicholas could now be styled 'Blessed Nicholas Owen'.

It was felt by many that the most deserving of those beatified should be formally advanced to the ranks of the Saints. The hierarchy of England and Wales entrusted the submission to the Jesuit Father Paolo Molinari and after much work by his assistants in England, Fathers Philip Caraman (to whom this book is dedicated) and James Walsh, a list of forty of those martyred in the persecution, including Nicholas, was submitted to Rome in 1960: this group being referred to as 'The Forty Martyrs of England and Wales'.[15]

Catholics are encouraged not only to pray to the saints, but also to ask them to intercede with God for their own intentions, and it is normally required that before a person is declared a Saint, two miracles have to be attributed to such prayers. Many cases were put forward in which the recipient believed an event was due to his or her prayers to the Forty Martyrs; and out of these, twenty-four were forwarded to the Congregation of Rites as seemingly miraculous. In turn, the Congregation submitted the evidence to medical and other experts for examination and two cases were selected as being most striking. These were the cure of a young mother, Joan Matthewman, from a cancerous tumour and the cure of a young girl, Teresa Hynes, from a pancreatic illness.

Martyrs have traditionally been accorded some indulgence by the Church, and in fact Thomas More and John Fisher who were martyred very early in the persecution were given a dispensation on this score and were canonised without evidence of miraculous intervention. Having regard to this precedent, the Pope gave permission for the canonisation process to proceed on the basis of the Matthewman case alone.[16]

A short time later, in May 1970, Pope Paul VI was able to declare that Nicholas and his companions were to be enrolled among the saints. This took place on the 25th October of that year at St Peter's in Rome in a ceremony extending over twenty-one hours. During Holy Communion, while the Crimond setting of 'The Lord's my Shepherd' was sung, a number of people received the host from Pope Paul himself; these included some descendants of the martyrs, and Teresa Hynes, then ten years old.[17]

Following revision of the liturgy, the feast day of the Forty Martyrs is now celebrated on the 4th May, and Nicholas has his own specific feast day on the 22nd March.

The painting opposite was commissioned by the General Postulation of the Society of Jesus to mark the occasion. Nicholas is shown kneeling in the foreground and in the background is the Tower of London where he died. This painting now hangs at Stonor Park, Oxfordshire, once the headquarters of Edmund Campion.

Once canonised, it is permissible for churches and altars in sidechapels to be dedicated to the saint. There are now many altars and a number of churches dedicated to the Forty Martyrs and two churches dedicated specifically to Nicholas Owen. One of these is in Northamptonshire, not far from where he had his narrow escape at Kirby Hall.

Of the persons mentioned in this story, Edmund Campion and Robert Southwell are also among the Forty Martyrs. Edward Oldcorne and his servant Ralph Ashley were among those declared

The Forty Martyr-Saints of England and Wales
by Daphne Pollen (courtesy CBCEW)

Blessed in 1929, but were not put forward as candidates for canonisation. Henry Garnet, who was the Jesuit Superior and who also
died for his faith, has received no formal recognition. Although his
name was among those submitted to the Congregation of Rites in
the nineteenth century, his Cause was not permitted to proceed.[18]
We can only guess at the reasons for this, but the basic requirement
for both beatification and canonisation is that the candidate has
displayed 'heroic virtue'. That is, he or she has not only constantly
performed virtuous actions but has done them joyfully and without
thought for the worldly consequences. It is clear from his writings
that this cannot be said of Henry Garnet. He constantly refers to the
fate that awaited him on capture. As early as 1586 his reputation for
fortitude was so low that the students at Douai mocked him as 'a
little wretch of a man, who day and night thinks of nothing save the
rack and the gibbet.'[19] Garnet worked constantly for the Church and
always did his duty but in the end this is not enough for the highest
honours.

In his book on hiding places, Granville Squiers gives us his vision
of Owen: 'It is not difficult to visualise a sturdy, taciturn little man,
limping his way to some lonely mansion with a pack of tools on his
back.'[20] This is a compelling description, but I feel it to be less than

accurate. Gerard praised his skill at negotiating with landlords so rather than being taciturn he must have been at ease in conversation to discuss business matters and generally recommend himself. Also we know from the *Narrative* that when he broke his leg he made himself loved by the people at the inn during his enforced stay. This would hardly be the case if he had been merely polite, so rather than being solitary he must have been able to make friends easily. He was also known to be very intelligent; the author of the *Narrative* saying:

> the contriving of his works in the safest manner were also very much assisted by an extraordinary wit and discretion which he had in such measure as I have seldom in my life seen the like in a man of his quality, which is also the opinion of most that did know him well.[21]

We have then a picture of an intelligent and companionable man who was also a skilled and knowledgeable craftsman. The writer also praises his piety, saying:

> I think no man can say that in all that seventeen or eighteen years they heard him swear by any oath, or ever saw him out of charity; yea, I have heard his ghostly [spiritual] Fathers affirm very seriously, that in all that time they never knew him to have committed mortal sin, nor anything that might be doubted to be such. His practice of the chiefest virtues was such that he had gotten great habits both in the religious virtues of poverty, chastity, and obedience, and no less in humility, patience, and charity, which upon all occasions were very plainly seen in his conversation and actions, insomuch that he was as a pattern of those virtues in every house where he came.[22]

This chapter of the *Narrative* concludes with the petition: 'In the meantime I desire my soul may have part with his, and myself may be assisted with his holy prayers.'[23] In other words, the writer hopes for Nicholas' prayers from heaven. In the Italian version of the manuscript the chapter ends before this point so these must be Father Gerard's own words, and is a remarkable thing for a Jesuit priest to say of a humble layman.

In the end what raised him to sainthood was not his martyrdom alone, but also his loyalty to his friends, his unstinting labours for his Church and his faith that gave him the strength to endure unto death tortures which can surely be compared to those of the Cross.

Sources

Much of the information in this book is taken from Father John Gerard's account of his apostolate in England, a work which is commonly known as his *Autobiography*. The original was written in Latin and several translations have appeared over the years. An accessible version with notes is *The Autobiography of a Hunted Priest*, (Ignatius Press, 2012) translated by Philip Caraman. Gerard also translated into English a report on the events of 1605/6, a work which is known as the *Narrative of the Gunpowder Plot*, or simply the *Narrative*. These two manuscripts were issued as a single volume in 1872 under the title *The Conditions of Catholics Under James I*, edited and translated by John Morris. This has been recently reprinted (Forgotten Books, 2012). References in the text to the *Autobiography* and the *Narrative* are to the two parts of this book.

Much has also been taken from the letters of Henry Garnet to his superiors in Rome and to others. These are held in the Archives of the British Province of the Society of Jesus, abbreviated here to ABSI.

For more details about the milieu in which Nicholas moved, the two works above together with Philip Caraman's biography of Henry Garnet, *Henry Garnet 1555–1606 and the Gunpowder Plot* (Longmans, 1964), cover most of the ground.

For more information on the activities and fates of the missionary priests of that time, the reader is referred to Alice Hogge's *God's Secret Agents* (Harper Perennial, 2005).

The last years of Nicholas' life were dominated by the drama of

149

the Gunpowder Plot. Many books have been written about this, but a popular modern work which is more sympathetic to the plotter's motives than most is Lady Antonia Fraser's *The Gunpowder Plot – Terror and Faith in 1605* (Phoenix, 2002).

For those interested in the history and details of priest-holes the standard work is *Secret Hiding Places* by Michael Hodgetts, (Veritas Publications, 1989).

Chapter Notes

Chapter 1 - Young Nicholas

1. Calendar of State Papers, James I. vol. 14 no. 216/153 (reprinted in *Worcs. Recusant* 47 [June 1986] p. 28).
2. Nichols, John Gouge, ed., *Literary Remains of King Edward VI.* (1857) vol. 2, p. 228.
3. Calendar of State Papers, Spain (Simancas), vol. 1: 1558–67 (1892), pp. 217–22.
4. Henry Garnet to Claudio Aquaviva, 25 May 1590. ABSI. 651, f.83.
5. Miscellaneous Volume, A.5.3. *Inrolment of Apprentices 1514–1591*, p. 278. Oxford City Archives.
6. Pollard, A.F. *Tudor Tracts.* (1903), p. 462.
7. Hargrave, Francis. *A Complete Collection of State-Trials and Proceedings for High Treason.* (1776), p. 1611.
8. Calendar of State Papers, Elizabeth. vol. 155, no. 42.
9. Caraman, Philip, trans. *The Autobiography of a Hunted Priest.* (2012), p. 6.
10. More, Henry. *Historia Missionis Anglicanae.* (1660), p. 31.
11. Henry Garnet to Claudio Aquaviva, 16 April 1596. ABSI. 651, ff.143–6.
12. Carter, Harry. *A History of the Oxford University Press.* (1975), pp. 17–22.
13. Harmsen, T.H.B.M. *John Gee's Foot Out of the Snare.* (1624), (The Cicero Press, Nijmegen, 1992) p. 241.
14. Caraman, Philip. *Henry Garnet.* (1964), p. 48.
15. Caraman, Philip, trans. *The Autobiography of a Hunted Priest.* (2012), p. 253.
16. *Narrative*, p. 182.

Chapter 2 - The Bloody Question

1. Catholic Truth Society. *The Martyrs of England and Wales, 1535–1680.* (1979), pp. 11–16.
2. Henry Garnet to Claudio Aquaviva, 26 August 1587. ABSI. 651, ff.55–57.
3. Caraman, Philip. *William Weston.* (1955), p. 45.

4. Allen, William. *An admonition to the nobility and people of England and Ireland* (Antwerp 1588).
5. Robert Southwell to Claudio Aquaviva, 31 August 1588. McCoog, Thomas. *And Touching our Society* (2013), p. 172.
6. Henry Garnet to Claudio Aquaviva, 17 March 1594. ABSI. SC, Anglia I, 73.
7. Caraman, Philip, trans. *The Autobiography of a Hunted Priest.* (2012), p. 90.
8. Henry Garnet to Robert Persons, 4 October 1605. Tierney, M.A. *Dodd's Church History of England.* (1841) vol. IV, Appendix, p. cii.

Chapter 3 - Refuge

1. Caraman, Philip. *Henry Garnet.* (1964), p. 97.
2. Henry Garnet to Claudio Aquaviva, 13 September 1590. ABSI. 651, f. 85.
3. Henry Garnet to Claudio Aquaviva, 17 March 1594. ABSI. SC, Anglia I, 73.
4. *Ibid.*
5. Autobiography, p. 39.
6. *Ibid.*
7. Henry Garnet to Claudio Aquaviva, 17 March 1594. ABSI. SC, Anglia I, 73.
8. *Ibid.*
9. *Ibid.*
10. Autobiography, p. 52.
11. *Ibid.,* p. 53.
12. *Ibid.,* p. 54.
13. *Ibid.,* p. 55.
14. *Ibid.,* p. 56.

Chapter 4 - Arrest

1. Henry Garnet to Claudio Aquaviva, 18 October 1591. ABSI. 651, f. 89.
2. Henry Garnet to Claudio Aquaviva, 11 February 1592. ABSI. 651, f. 91.
3. Henry Garnet to Claudio Aquaviva, 16 July 1592. ABSI. 651, f. 94
4. *Narrative,* p. 18.
5. *Autobiography,* p. 61.
6. Henry Garnet to Claudio Aquaviva, 16 July 1592. ABSI. 651, f. 94.
7. *Ibid.*
8. Richard Vestegan to Roger Baynes, 1 August 1592. Catholic Record Society, vol. 52, p. 51.
9. Richard Vestegan to Robert Persons, 15 October 1592. Catholic Record Society, vol. 52, p. 79.
10. Richard Vestegan to Robert Persons, 1592. Catholic Record Society, vol. 52, p. 97.
11. Richard Vestegan to Robert Persons, 15 October 1592. Catholic Record Society, vol. 52, p. 79.
12. Richard Vestegan to Robert Persons, 1592. Catholic Record Society, vol. 52, p. 97.
13. British Library. Lansdowne MS 72/39.

14. Janelle, Pierre. *Robert Southwell The Writer.* (1971) p. 66.
15. Henry Garnet to Claudio Aquaviva, 16 July 1592. ABSI. 651, f. 94.
16. Claudio Aquaviva to Henry Garnet, 9 January 1593. Arch. S. J. Rome, Fland. Belg. 1, f. 109.
17. Caraman, Philip, trans. *The Autobiography of a Hunted Priest.* (2012), p. 78.
18. *Autobiography*, p. 43.
19. Calendar of State Papers, Elizabeth. vol. 248, no. 103.
20. Caraman, Philip. *Henry Garnet.* (1964), p. 188.
21. Calendar of State Papers, Elizabeth. vol. 248, no. 103.
22. *Autobiography*, p. 65.
23. *Ibid.*, p. 61 n.
24. *Ibid.*, p. 60.
25. Ward, Ned. *The London Spy.* (1993) p. 69 .
26. Tierney, M.A. *Dodd's Church History of England.* (1841) Appendix 34.
27. Henry Garnet to Claudio Aquaviva, 22 February 1595. ABSI. SC, Anglia II, 13.
28. Fraser, Lady Antonia. *The Gunpowder Plot: Terror and Faith in 1605.* (2002), p. 41.

Chapter 5 – Escape from the Tower

1. Law, Thomas Graves. *Collected Essays and Reviews.* (1904), p. 154.
2. Henry Garnet to Claudio Aquaviva, 16 April 1596. ABSI. SC, Anglia 31, ff. 127–32.
3. *Autobiography*, p. 97.
4. *Ibid.*, p. 102.
5. *Ibid.*, p. 118.
6. *Ibid.*, p. 120.
7. *Ibid.*, p. 121.
8. *Ibid.*, p. 123.
9. *Ibid.*
10. Morris, John, ed. *The Troubles of Our Catholic Forefathers.* First Series, (1872), p. 177.
11. Roberts, R. A., ed. *Calendar of the Cecil Papers in Hatfield House* (1883) vol. 7, 5 Oct. 1597.
12. *Autobiography*, p. 176.
13. Morris, John, ed. *The Troubles of Our Catholic Forefathers.* First Series, (1872), p. 180.
14. *Autobiography*, p. 162.
15. *Narrative*, p. 188.
16. *Ibid.*, p. 185.

Chapter 6 – The Gunpowder Plot

1. Henry Garnet to Robert Persons 16 April 1603. Tierney, M.A. *Dodd's Church History of England.* (1841) vol. 4, p. 64.
2. Williams, E. C. *Anne of Denmark.* (1970), p. 200.
3. Bruce, John, ed. *Correspondence of James VI with Sir Robert Cecil and others in England.* Camden Society (1861), p. 36.
4. Jardine, David. *Criminal Trials.* vol. II, The Gunpowder Plot. (1832), p. 19.
5. Ellis, Henry. *Original Letters Illustrative of English History,* (1827), 2nd Series, iii, Letter CCXLIX.
6. Akrigg, G. P. V., ed. *Letters of King James VI and I* (1984), p. 78.
7. *Narrative,* p. 25.
8. Jardine, David. *Criminal Trials.* vol. II, The Gunpowder Plot. (1832) p. 159.
9. Fraser, Lady Antonia. *The Gunpowder Plot: Terror and Faith in 1605.* (2002), p. 117 and Hogge, Alice. *God's Secret Agents.* (2006), p. 332.
10 Jardine, David. *Criminal Trials.* vol. II, The Gunpowder Plot. (1832), p. 150.
11. *Ibid.,* p. 158.
12. *Ibid.,* p. 160.
13. *Narrative,* p. 53.
14. Calendar of State Papers, James I. vol. 20, no. 45.
15. *Narrative,* p. 71.
16. Caraman, Philip. *Henry Garnet.* (1964), p. 318.
17. Henry Garnet to Claudio Aquaviva 15 June 1605. Tierney, M.A. *Dodd's Church History of England.* (1841) vol. 4, Appendix 58.
18. Hatfield House, the Cecil Papers 110/30, reprinted in English Historical Review, vol. 3 (1888), p. 512.
19. *Ibid.,* pp. 513–4.
20. *Ibid.,* p. 514.
21. Calendar of State Papers, James I. vol. 14, no. 216/153 (reprinted in Worcs. Recusant 47 [June 1986] p. 28).
22. Weldon, Anthony. *The Court and Character of King James.* (1651), p. 55.
23. Sidney, Philip. *A History of the Gunpowder Plot.* (1904), pp. 240–2.
24. Foley, Henry. *Records of the English Province of the Society of Jesus.* vol. 4 (1877), p. 145.
25. *Ibid.,* p. 107.
26. Calendar of State Papers, James I. vol. 19, no. 16.
27. *Ibid.*

Chapter 7 – Capture

1. Britton, J. and Laird, F.C. *Beauties of England and Wales.* vol. 15, Part I, (1814), p. 184.
2. Taunton, Ethelred L., *The History of the Jesuits in England 1580–1773.* (1901), p. 303.
3. Morris, John. *The Life of Father John Gerard.* (1881) p. 119.

4. Roberts, R. A., ed. *Calendar of the Cecil Papers in Hatfield House.* vol. 6, July 17, 1596.
5. Calendar of State Papers, James I. vol. 18, no. 29.
6. Edwards, Francis. "The Stonyhurst Narratives of the Gunpowder Plot". *Journal of the Society of Archivists* vol. 4, Issue 2, 1970.
7. Tesimond, Oswald. *The Gunpowder Plot: The Narrative of Oswald Tesimond alias Greenway.* (1973), p. 94 and *Narrative*, p. 183.
8. British Library. Harley MS 360, ff. 92–108.
9. Calendar of State Papers, James I, vol. 25, no. 38.
10. *Narrative*, p. 151.
11. Tesimond, Oswald. *The Gunpowder Plot: The Narrative of Oswald Tesimond alias Greenway.* (1973), p. 165.
12. *Narrative*, p. 151.
13. Calendar of State Papers, James I. vol. 18, no. 38.
14. *Narrative*, p. 153.
15. Calendar of State Papers, James I. vol. 18, no. 38.
16. Daybell, James. *The Material Letter in Early Modern England.* (2012) p. 118.
17. Jardine, David. *Criminal Trials.* vol. II, The Gunpowder Plot. (1832), p. 167n.
18. *Narrative*, p. 153.
19. *Ibid.*, p. 152.
20. Calendar of State Papers, James I. vol. 19, no. 11.
21. *Ibid.*

Chapter 8 – The Hides

1. Squiers, Granville. *Secret Hiding Places.* (1933), p. 202.
2. *Narrative*, p. 182.
3. *Ibid.*, p. 183.
4. *Ibid.*, p. 184.
5. Tesimond, Oswald. *The Gunpowder Plot: The Narrative of Oswald Tesimond alias Greenway.* (1973), p.194.
6. *Autobiography*, p. 158.
7. Squiers, Granville. *Secret Hiding Places.* (1933), p. 25.
8. Caraman, Philip. *Henry Garnet.* (1964), p. 96.
9. Squiers, Granville. *Secret Hiding Places.* (1933), p. 87.
10. *Narrative*, p.184.
11. Morris, John, ed. *The Troubles of our Catholic Forefathers.* First Series, (1872), pp. 207–11.
12. Robert Southwell to Claudio Aquaviva, 28 December 1588. Printed in McCoog, Thomas. *And Touching our Society.* (2013), pp. 188–92.
13. Hodgetts, Michael. Elizabethan Priest Holes IV – Harvington. *Recusant History*, vol. 13 (1975), p. 50.
14. Hodgetts, Michael. *Secret Hiding Places.* (1989), p. 126.
15. Calendar of State Papers, James I. vol. 18, no. 29.

16. *Narrative*, p. 37.
17. Hodgetts, Michael. Elizabethan Priest-Holes IV – Harvington. *Recusant History*, vol. 13 (1975), p. 42.

Chapter 9 – Torture and Death

1. *Narrative*, p. 186.
2. Tesimond, Oswald. *The Gunpowder Plot: The Narrative of Oswald Tesimond alias Greenway*, (1973), p. 198.
3. *Narrative*, p. 169.
4. Calendar of State Papers, James I. vol. 18, no. 117 .
5. The Duke of Norfolk. *The Lives of Philip Howard, Earl of Arundel and of Anne Dacres, his Wife* (1857), p. 115.
6. Sir Thomas Smith. *De Republica Anglorum*. (1583), p. 105.
7. Dasent, John Roche, ed. *Acts of the Privy Council in England*. (1890), vol. 27, p. 38.
8. *Report of the Royal Commission on Historical Manuscripts*. (2012), Issue 12, Part 1, p. 60.
9. *Narrative*. p. 188.
10. Calendar of State Papers, James I. vol. 18, Feb. 26.
11. *Narrative*, p.188.
12. Tesimond, Oswald. *The Gunpowder Plot: The Narrative of Oswald Tesimond alias Greenway*, (1973), p. 198.
13. *Ibid.*, p. 201.
14. *Narrative*, p. 188.
15. Calendar of State Papers, James I. vol. 19, March 1.
16. *Narrative*, p. 189.
17. Caraman, Philip. *Saint Nicholas Owen, Maker of Hiding Holes.* (1980), p. 16.
18. Jardine, David. *Criminal Trials*. vol. II, The Gunpowder Plot. (1832), p.109.
19. Calendar of State Papers, James I. vol. 19, no. 94.
20. Abbott, Dr. Robert. *Antilogia*. (1613), p. 114.
21. *Narrative*, p. 186.
22. Bartoli, Daniello. *Dell'istoria della Compagnia di Gesù l'Inghilterra*. (1667), p. 542.
23. British Library, Stowe MS 168, f. 364r.
24. Proceedings of the Court of Star Chamber. STAC 8/5/16.
25. Calendar of State Papers, Venetian. vol. 10, pp. 327–28.
26. Bartoli, Daniello. *Dell'istoria della Compagnia di Gesù l'Inghilterra*. (1667), p. 542.
27. *Ibid.*
28. Narrative, p. 188.
29. Catholic Record Society, vol. 60, p. 134.
30. Catholic Record Society, vol. 34, p. 5. See also, Harmsen, T.H.B.M. *John Gee's Foot Out of the Snare*. (1624), (The Cicero Press, Nijmegen, 1992), p. 241.

31. *Narrative*, p. 189.
32. *Ibid.*, p. 188.
33. *Ibid.*
34. *Ibid.*, p. 187.
35. *Ibid.*, p. 188.

Chapter 10 – The Forty Martyrs

1. More, Henry. *Historia Provinciae Anglicanae.* (1660), p. 322.
2. *Narrative*, p. 290.
3. *Ibid.*, p. 295.
4. "Rare book 'bears image of hanged priest's face'" *The Guardian*, 27 November 2007.
5. Calendar of State Papers, James I, vol. 18, no. 19.
6. Harmsen, T.H.B.M. *John Gee's Foot Out of the Snare.* (1624), (The Cicero Press, Nijmegen, 1992), p. 241.
7. Tanner, Mathias. *Societas Jesu usque ad Sanguinis et Vitae Profusionem Militans.* (1675), p. 73.
8. Foley, Henry. *Records of the English Province of the Society of Jesus*, vol. 4 (1877), p. 246.
9. McCoog, Thomas. *The Society of Jesus in Ireland, Scotland and England 1541–88.* (2012) p. 142.
10. *Narrative*, p.185.
11. Henry Garnet to Claudio Aquaviva, 7 November 1599. ABSI. 651, f.110.
12. Henry Garnet to Robert Persons 4 October 1605. Tierney, M.A. *Dodd's Church History of England.* (1841) vol. IV, Appendix, p. cii.
13. Wolffe, John. *God and Greater Britain.* (1994), p. 31.
14. Acta Apolstolicae Sedis, 22 (1930), pp. 34–37.
15. Molinari, Paolo. "Canonization of 40 English and Welsh Martyrs". *L'Osservatore Romano*, 29 October 1970.
16. "Compendium Vitae Martyrii ac Miraculorum". *Archivio Postulazione Generale.* 963/46 (1970).
17. "The Martyrs are now the Saints". *Catholic Herald*, Thursday 30 Oct 1970.
18. McCoog, Thomas. "Remembering Henry Garnet" *Archivum Historicum Societatis Jesu*, Jan-June 2006.
19. Caraman, Philip. *Henry Garnet.* (1964), p. 207.
20. Squiers, Granville. *Secret Hiding Places.* (1933), p. 25.
21. *Narrative*, p. 184.
22. *Ibid.*
23. *Ibid.*, p. 190.

Index